Hilton U. Brown III

D0046314

GOING LIGHT—WITH BACKPACK OR BURRO

Going Light

edited by DAVID R. BROWN

vith backpack or burro

th contributions by
Lewis F. Clark, Elizabeth Cowles,
Alex Hildebrand, Joel H. Hildebrand,
Milton Hildebrand, Mildred Jentsch Bennett,
Louise H. Klein, H. Stewart Kimball (M.D.),
Richard M. Leonard, Bestor Robinson

illustrated by MILTON HILDEBRAND

SIERRA CLUB
SAN FRANCISCO

PUBLISHED ON THE YNES MEXÍA PUBLICATIONS FUND

The Sierra Club, founded in 1892 by John Muir, invites
participation in its program—a program that needs continuing and
wide support—to preserve the nation's scenic resources,
including wilderness, wildlife, forests, and streams.
Address: Mills Tower, San Francisco 4

Eighth printing, 1964
Copyright 1951 by the Sierra Club
Designed by David Brower
Manufactured in the United States of America
by the Vail-Ballou Press, Inc., Binghamton, N.Y.

to those who walk

the sky-land trails

Foreword

SO YOU ARE going to the mountains? Here is a book on how to plan to hit the trail. It will serve you well as a guide to full enjoyment of America's rich heritage of high country.

Going Light has been written by backpackers seasoned on the trails of mountain parks and forests. City dwellers who have been timid about going into the back country beyond the roads, will be encouraged by those who have put their experience into this book, including their discovery of the joys of traveling light.

The contributors, the editor, and the Sierra Club deserve our gratitude for their design of *Going Light*. You travelers who have reached the foothills and just discovered the trails leading to the mountains will find this book a companion that will lighten your pack as you travel to timberline and beyond. Officials charged with the responsibilities of protecting your trail country will welcome *Going Light* as an aid in helping visitors to live right in the mountains.

NEWTON B. DRURY

Washington, D.C.
January 8, 1951

Preface

IT WAS IN Joel Hildebrand's garden in Berkeley that this book was born. A group of us had gathered on a fogless spring evening for a friendly discussion of this and that. Newton Drury, then Director of the National Park Service, was what you might consider the guest of honor, and it was only natural that in the course of the evening there should be several suggestions on how to run the national parks.

The tide of talk flowed naturally to Yosemite—as it always does when Californians who like mountains get together—and before it ebbed we had thought long and hard about the fatal beauty of Yosemite, of the overcrowding that resulted from that beauty, of what could be done there and in other parks equally popular to protect the beauty from the throngs it attracted. A garden will withstand an occasional errant footprint but not a million, and Yosemite was periodically taking a beating from the crowds that might number 30,000 on a Fourth of July week end and could not be contained on the roads, the roadsides, the near-by trails, in the hotels, or in the campgrounds. The park rangers could no longer range; they had to be called in to police traffic. Others who served the public saw so much public they tired of it a little. Visitors who came to enjoy urban pleasures in a new environment found the lines of like visitors too long, and visitors who came just to see Yosemite for itself saw more of other visitors than of Yosemite.

The usual enterprising solution, to expand to meet the demand, would hardly work here; the size of Yosemite Valley was pretty well predetermined. It would hardly help to improve the road so that people could drive in and out the same day, and thus circulate through, rather than be precipitated in, the valley. But something would some day have to be done, that we were agreed; something relatively drastic, against the day when the population of the West became denser than now and its recreational needs greater.

None of those discussing these things was worried for himself. We knew where in Yosemite we could go, even on a Fourth of July week end, in order not to have our toes stepped on. It was simply a matter of arithmetic. The crowd diminished according to the square of the distance from the highway and according to the cube of the elevation above it. Thus, no matter what the crowd, the rock climbers had no problem at all. The Cathedral Spires were all theirs. Those who preferred their off-highway strolls a little less perpendicular could do very well on any of the trails except those nearest the hotels and perhaps the first two miles of the trail to Vernal and Nevada falls. We knew for sure that no matter what the valley-floor crowd, it was possible to travel all day on almost any of the trails in the Yosemite High Sierra without meeting more than a few people.

It was clear that for at least the crowded summer season the real Yosemite—the serene mood of the parkland—would have to be sought well beyond the Sierra roads and highways. It also became clear that a service could be rendered to those who really wanted to experience that mood if we could compile a book that would explain how simply, how inexpensively, and how enjoyably they might get into the back country—whether in Yosemite or in the other western national parks, national forests, national monuments, state parks, or even into whatever private lands might still be primitive enough to provide the challenge of the wilderness.

We resolved, then, to put this little book together. We were not anxious to overadvertise how satisfying the back country can be; for then it, too, might suffer the fate of summertime Yosemite. But we are not too troubled. We are well aware how unlikely it is that any mere book would lure in excessive numbers from the throttle the housebound citizen to whom a night in the open, on rather uncompromising ground, under the stars or under the clouds, is repulsive. But we hope that somehow these pages will stimulate and encourage those who feel they should like to be up there—up where the trails are. And we're anxious not only that they be encouraged to seek, but also that they be persuaded to protect to the utmost, the wild places they have sought—and lived with and loved.

DAVID R. BROWER

Berkeley, California
February 15, 1951

More than a decade later (and six printings later, each helped by suggestions from readers), the book is still at it. The need seems even greater in these days of ubiquitous attempts to move the wilderness experience to the roadside. True wilderness is where you keep it, and real wilderness experience cannot be a sedentary one; you have to seek it out—not seated, but afoot. That, at least, is how the Sierra Club feels about it.

D. R. B.

Berkeley, August 1, 1962

Acknowledgments

IT IS ALWAYS a little hard, when a book such as this has been compiled, to identify accurately the work of each of the contributors. At one time or another, each has looked over the drafts of the others and has added his own bit to them. It is easy, however, and a pleasant duty, to say who has done the main work on the chapters and who is therefore responsible for the good that is in them: Lewis F. Clark, part of chapter 3; Elizabeth Cowles, chapter 10; Alex Hildebrand, chapter 5; Joel Hildebrand, chapters 1 and 3; Milton Hildebrand, chapters 3, 12, 13; Mildred Jentsch, the special food list; Louise H. Klein, chapters 9 and 11; H. Stewart Kimball, M.D., chapter 8; Richard M. Leonard, chapters 4 and 7; Bestor Robinson, chapter 6.

To these people, then, the credit—and special credit to the Hildebrands for skillful revising and counsel. To the editor the responsibility for the final judgments passed after the others had had their last look at the manuscript —and for not subduing his predilections (if any should happen to have survived so many scrutinies).

Grateful acknowledgment is also due many friends for their encouragement, the University of California Press for permission to borrow parts of the *Manual of Ski Mountaineering,* and to each reader who helps make future editions more complete.

D. R. B.

Contents

[xiii]

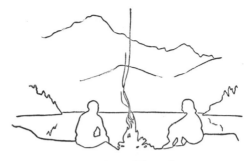

1. Open House on the Trail

The outer world, from which we cower into our houses, seemed after all a gentle, habitable place; and night after night a man's bed, it seemed, was laid and waiting for him in fields, where God keeps an open house. I thought I had rediscovered one of those truths which are revealed to savages and hid from political economists: at the least, I had discovered a new pleasure for myself.

Travels with a Donkey—R. L. Stevenson

THIS BOOK IS written for a special sort of person, one not completely civilized, a throwback to an early age when man lived close to nature—his enemy if he were ignorant or slothful, his friend if he were observant, ingenious, self-reliant, and tough. Those who retain an atavistic residue like to give up the luxuries of civilization from time to time and to go on a sort of spree, during which they deliberately substitute legs for wheels, muscles for motors, pine-needle beds for spring mattresses, moon and stars for neon lights, singing birds for ringing tele-

[1]

phones, campfires for radiators, and glowing embers for a TV screen. There are people, of course, who cannot comprehend any such voluntary surrender of civilized comforts; people who see a mountain chiefly as an obstacle to a highway, or a desert as worthless real estate; people who buy their fun instead of making it.

You are not that sort of person or you wouldn't have opened this book; but if you are and have opened it by mistake, put it down at once, for you will not enjoy it, unless, perhaps, to laugh at us queer ones who find hiking a pleasure. This is compiled for people who have the instinct to hit the trail, but have either never known how to get beyond the lunch-box stage, or, having ventured farther, would like to learn more. There is much to learn.

A basic fact of life that especially impresses itself upon the hiker is that you pay in one way or another for everything you get. If the backpacker takes along an air mattress in order to be more comfortable at night, it makes him uncomfortable all day long as it pulls at his shoulders. And, if, instead, he decides to let a burro carry this and other comforts, the animal brings along his own peculiar problems. If you want good fishing, you may have to go where there are mosquitoes as well as fish. If you want to camp amid the inspiring scenery of timberline, your nights will be cold. This is a fine lesson to learn and willingly accept, for these are only the just prices that have to be paid for the good things of life—prices that have not been inflated by greed.

It helps to realize that there are several methods of trail travel, each offering its own particular advantages in return for its own natural costs. The backpack trip is the cheapest in money and the freest as to movement and campsites. It enables one to take routes that animals cannot travel. It frees one from the necessity of reserving animals long in advance. Its disadvantages are, first, that even the minimum pack becomes heavy on trips longer than a week or ten days by reason of the irreducible limit of about two pounds of food per day, unless one has a hump on which to live. Second, the heavy pack urges one to hurry along to the next resting point instead of sauntering along the trail and looking about. And, third, you cannot take your very young family very far on a backpack trip, and, while waiting for them to grow up, you may grow sedentary and flabby. It pays, therefore, to learn how to pack burros. A child of four can ride a burro, and a child of one and a half can be carried on his dad's back as described later in this book—provided that dad knows how to pack the duffle on a burro or two. When the family grows up, mules may be taken instead of burros for faster travel, fewer animals per party, and less trouble on difficult trails crossing snowfields and streams. A good burro is a wise little beast of burden that soon becomes a pet if properly treated; and a mule is one of the noblest creations of man (not of God), intelligent, powerful, and made for mountain travel.

Every hiker awakens early to some of the rewards of trail and camp, but the potential rewards are so numerous that he may overlook others which would increase the richness of the experience. There are some who appear to go out only for trout. Trout are not to be despised, whether on the end of a line or in a frying pan, but some fishermen seem to have no other source of enjoyment. Yet the trail offers much besides a route to a trout stream. The rocks, the trees, the flowers, the animals and birds, and the landscape, all invite attention. A person who can see in the sculpture of the terrain the geologic history of the region has a great drama unfolded before him; one who can name the trees and the wildflowers has a pleasure similar to that of meeting friends; one who becomes for a time a member of the wildlife community rather than an intruder can enjoy the sense of belonging in good society. The photographer has an infinite choice of unhackneyed material for fine pictures instead of just snapshots. Nor should we neglect to mention one of the greatest satisfactions of all—of being able to concoct an apple pie, or a special mulligan, or hot nut-date biscuits that elicit such appreciation as only the combination of good cooking and trail appetites can arouse.

And, finally, there is no activity that can contribute more to the development of certain important elements of character. Parents who take to the trail with their children are not likely to have serious problems of discipline, because the lessons of camp and trail are automatic and reasonable. Good humor, cooperation, control of emotion, are called forth in child and adult alike by their obvious value. And an adult whose sense of values has become distorted by city life gains a truer perspective in the presence of majestic mountains. Money and social prestige seem less essential to a person lying in his sleeping bag, with pleasantly tired muscles, looking up through the trees at such heavens as are never seen in the neighborhood of cities. But it is not necessary to take self-improvement too seriously, for all such moral benefits can be taken merely as by-products of the delight to be found by hitting the trail. Let's go!

2. About Camping

THE WILDERNESS AREAS of the national forests, the primitive, back-country regions of the national parks—these are the places where hitting the trail and camping out are going to be most enticing. To whom does this wilderness country, this land that must be lived in to be seen, belong? Not in title, of course; practically all of it is government-owned, and that means it belongs to everyone. But whose are these lands to enjoy? Do they belong just to "the aristocracy of the physically fit," as has occasionally been said?

To a degree yes. Not to any widely discriminatory degree, however. That millions of citizens have not yet left their cars to explore the country's wilderness is due chiefly to a gap in their education. Perhaps they started out with a certain love of small-boy pioneering in the wilds, but they were allowed to forget and to lose it, and to grow up just a little afraid of wild places. An army colonel tells of an experience with an infantry organization composed almost entirely of men from a large Eastern city. Certainly they had not been timid in their customary environ-

[5]

ment, but the first time a field exercise required them to spend a night out in the woods an amazing number of them wept. An Air Force officer tells a sadder story of a pilot who was forced down an easy day's walk from civilization in the north woods but who, for fear of the unknown of the wilderness, shot himself in the few hours before rescuers reached him.

These may be overdramatic examples of the failure to learn about living in the wilderness. Other, everyday examples are implicit in what many a man has learned to think of as proper traveling. A proper traveler, he feels, must travel far. If he can't afford Europe, then certainly the least he should aspire to is to do the national parks— probably doing all of them in a single summer. He wheels them by in rapid succession. So long as his timing allows him to pass by Old Faithful in eruption, he has seen Yellowstone. A two-hour valley tour by car does Yosemite. Yes, he would like to get out of his car to stretch a bit and revive what the cushions have numbed, but there isn't time; there are two more parks in this particular state, and he has to take them in. He travels fast and far—never getting close to the ground or intimate with the terrain.

We want to emphasize here and now, even to the point of being evangelical in our emphasis, that one gains a great deal by getting just as far from exhaust fumes and ringing telephones as his feet will let him; that feet are the readiest means of access to such sanctuary; and that so long as one can walk, if only a mile or two a day, it is possible to use the wilderness as a sanctuary.

You are not too old. The Sierra Club, to choose the example we know best, has been running wilderness outings into the mountains since 1901, and the age range of those who have gone on the trips—walking all the way and sleeping on the ground—has been from eight to eighty.

You are not too young. Some children have started out, as side loads on a burro, before their first year was done. Among them were some who liked their indoctrination so well that they are now doing the same for their own children and have helped write a book about it—this book.

You are not of too frail a sex. Wilderness travel and pleasure is by no means for the hardy male alone. If you think so, or if you don't think so but your husband does, see the chapters on Women and Especially for Men.

Nor are you too poor. If you can make your way to the roadhead, beyond which the wilderness begins, you can arrange your trip so conservatively as to get by for less than it costs to live at home.

No, the wilderness is not for any aristocracy. We believe instead—and for a chapterful of reasons—that it is of high importance to everybody as a sort of safety valve. It has in it a little of what a window box has for a crowded apartment, a garden for a home, a park for a city. But it has more, for these are all on the orderly, manicured side. Wilderness, given the chance, takes care of itself. We'd like enough people to know about it, whether or not they use it often, to make certain that our few remaining wilderness areas always have that chance.

When to go

One can camp out in any season, but it is during the summer when schools are closed and the weather is relatively warm and dry that most family outings are taken. Further increase in population, in leisure hours, and in ease of travel may some day require staggering the use of public camping places unless more recreational areas are soon added to the public domain; but today the wilderness still provides plenty of room for travel, and the chief problem is merely to select the part of summer that is most satisfactory. It is well to start by camping when it is easiest to do so, but no one season is best, and the camper will find it rewarding to vary the season of his outings.

In the high mountains of the West, June is beautifully alpine. There may be too much snow at high elevations. Streams are so high that fording presents real problems where foot bridges are not provided, and fishing is likely to be poor. There may even be a late snowstorm—late but light. Nightly freezes are to be expected. Warm clothing and waterproof footgear will probably be needed.

By July there is less snow, and streams are lower. Days will be pleasantly warm unless a prolonged series of thunderstorms should develop, and night temperatures are milder. Early flowers are well under way.

August is still drier and warmer. Late flowers are at their peak. Streams and lakes are lower, and fly fishing should be at its best. This is the most popular month for camping and packtrain operators, who are booked up well in advance.

By late September most of the flowers have gone, but there are more berries. Deciduous greens have changed to fall colors. The mountains are ready for the first snow of the coming winter season, and the traveler should not be surprised if he happens to share it. One of the most important items of equipment in this, the hunting season, is a red hat—unless one is traveling in a national park.

There is wide variation from region to region. The dry season is shorter in the Cascades than in the Sierra.

One can camp out on the deserts of the Southwest at any season; but from November until May, in the regions receiving heavy snowfall, camping technique and equipment must usually be those of the winter mountaineer. These are discussed in detail in the *Manual of Ski Mountaineering*.

Where to go

A map of the places the wilderness camper can explore
would be a map of the Western States, the Appalachian
Chain, and the north-woods country—wherever mountain
and forest wilderness exist, together or separately. Most
of the suitable wilderness country has been set aside as
national parks and forests, or as state parks. Continued
vigilance is required if it is to remain so. There are resources which were not important when these areas were
placed in the public domain but which have since increased in value, and economic development of some
may be thought to be necessary; however, the recreational
value of the lands will also increase with time, and the
question of what will remain for future generations should
be fully considered in determining whether or not such
lands should be started down the one-way road of ex-
ploitation.

Of all the nation's back country, the High Sierra wilderness, embracing Yosemite, Sequoia, and Kings Canyon
national parks and Toiyabe, Inyo, Sierra, and Sequoia
national forests, is the largest. It is also the most livable.
The infrequency of summer storms in California allows
some desert characteristics to reach even the highest elevations; but the heavy winter snowfall produced by the
few storms that do arrive provides year-around stream-
flow. The Canadian and Arctic-Alpine Life Zones are
charming, well-watered, open, fair-weather sky-lands.

In the Cascades of Oregon and Washington summer
snows are progressively deeper as one travels northward;
glaciers, which are mere vestiges in California, are there
active ice engines transporting the mountains seaward. The
prodigious rain forests, with their gigantic trees and with
dense waterloving undergrowth, await the camper in

Olympic National Park and elsewhere near the coast where they have not been destroyed by the logger's saw. The weather that makes the glaciers and rain forests possible is much in evidence, and the camper must equip himself accordingly. Timberline is at about 6,000 feet.

The Rocky Mountains provide abundant opportunity for short trips. Extended outings are somewhat discouraged by the numerous roads and mining developments and by the heavy use of range lands.

The canyons, mesas, and ruins of the Southwest are a fascinating challenge to the explorer, but there is less need for going light on desert trips, because most of them do not go far from highways or automobile trails. It should be pointed out, however, that the ability to get along with lightweight, compact equipment adds to the ease and comfort of automobile camping.

Wherever one may wish to go, he is confronted with a difficult choice. Should he see new country, or should he renew an old acquaintance. The person who never leaves the road will probably have no hesitation; he is likely to choose the first. The wilderness traveler, who becomes intimately acquainted with campsites, vistas, and summits may find it harder to make a choice. What could be finer than to spend one's life discovering which plan is more desirable!

Having discussed the when and where of going light, we ought to explain how. The short answer to this is: acquire the technique, the equipment, the company, the time, the physical conditioning—and take off.

The company and the time are up to you. We can only urge that you approach your chosen companions with enthusiasm for the venture and with a good map of possible itineraries, and that if you don't have the time, you ought to make it.

3 Wilderness Traveling

WILDERNESS TRAVELING is ordinarily accomplished by walking, and since all of us know how to walk, the novice is able to enjoy hiking without previous experience or schooling. However, there is much more to wilderness travel than merely picking them up and setting them down. Mastery of the technique of travel contributes much toward the efficiency and safety of a camping trip. Efficiency makes it possible to feel fit instead of finished at the end of the day. Safety brings confidence for the trips ahead, and satisfaction over those behind. Let us see what there is to the technique of wilderness travel.

Organization

When planning a camping trip, it is important that organization be considered. It is not suggested that a chain of command be established. Schedule and itinerary will probably be decided upon by popular vote, and if each member of the party will care for himself and his equip-

[11]

ment, and will lend a willing hand when there is a job to be done, no one need be a taskmaster. However, community equipment and some aspects of the party welfare may be neglected unless made the responsibility of a leader. Did anyone find out if there is a snake-bite kit in the party? Is anyone keeping track of the time so we can get back to camp before dark? Did anyone make sure the fire was out before we broke camp? Certainly! The leader has done these things.

A very small group of experienced campers need not designate a leader because each member will unconsciously make it his own responsibility to see that the trip progresses smoothly and safely. If the party is larger or less experienced, leadership may be rotated among the qualified persons, or the responsibility for cooking, packing, and breaking trail may be divided among specialists. However, it is usually desirable to recognize a permanent leader even though he may delegate certain responsibilities.

The leader will see that community equipment is provided and cared for. He may need to check the personal equipment of a novice to be sure that it is adequate. Off trail the leader will usually go first if the terrain is rough, or if route selection is difficult, or if it is necessary to control the pace. In camp he makes sure that fires are controlled and that the site is left clean for the next party. He keeps track of the whereabouts of party members, and in the event of an accident he takes charge.

It is well for the leader to understand that a definite lift is experienced by the person who travels first along the trail, and that there is a corresponding letdown to being last. The last person may have had trouble with equipment. If he paused for a drink or to ward off a threatened blister, it may be very hard for him to catch up. He may be peeved at the main party for going too fast, and at the same time feel guilty for holding it up. Too often the faster hikers wait until the rear guard catches up only to strike out again, refreshed by their pause, the moment the tired stragglers come into view. Considering the unity, morale, and pleasure of the party, the leader may urge a slow hiker to walk near the front of the line, or even to take the lead. He may suggest—with great tact—that some of the hiker's pack be distributed among the stronger members of the party. Where the route is clear and safe it is often desirable for the party to split temporarily into two or more groups traveling at different speeds in order to accommodate differences in preference of pace. In this event it is important that there be a clear understanding of route and rendezvous point. The leader should pause soon after the start of a day's travel to make sure that everyone's equipment is working well; thus he can prevent the cause of much straggling.

If the leader must be considerate, it follows that the others should consider his feelings as well. The leader has taken the responsibility for finding a good general route and a good specific route, for trying to set a good pace, for keeping a good many necessary details in mind. It is a sure road to unpopularity for any of those who follow to take shortcuts, to strike off on little competitive variations of their own, to walk on his heels, to pass him, or on the other hand to lag unnecessarily behind. Photography can make about as many momentary enemies on a trip as it makes fast friends back home. The man who himself does not see a good shot becomes impatient with the man who stops to take it, and the man who stops becomes fully as irked at the one who forges on.

There is no need to expand upon the application of the Golden Rule. Suffice it to say that failure to remember the rule is less likely to spoil the atmosphere down in civilization, with its diverse throngs, than up in the back country, where the very scarcity of individuals may reveal too harshly those few rough spots in the personality of each one—rough spots from which the smallness of the group permits little escape.

Solo travel

Solo travel is seldom advisable or necessary, and should never be undertaken without the permission of one's party, and unless others know the route and schedule, and the equipment which will be carried. This is the most important rule of mountain travel. A person might claim the privilege of risking his own life by going off and getting lost, but he has no right to put his companions to the immense trouble and anxiety of trying to find him. An accident can happen even to an experienced hiker. A sprained ankle could incapacitate him, and his life might depend upon whether his comrades know where to look for him. If solo travel is justified, the hiker should carry with him a little food, extra wraps, a flashlight, a map, and *matches*. He should avoid off-trail travel if possible.

Schedule

Unless the day's trip is to be short, it is usually best to start early and to camp early, to permit the selection of an attractive campsite and have time for fishing, botanizing, washing, fixing a soft bed, or cooking something extra special. Moreover, travel in the cool early hours of the day is by far the least wearing. The itinerary for the day should be decided upon before setting out in the morning, and each member of the party should know the plan.

Pace

It is good to be able to travel far and fast, and a party of young people often finds pleasure in the ability to do so. But there are also rewards to more leisurely travel which should not be overlooked. Go as fast as you can comfortably go—unless you feel impelled to break records.

The novice often starts the day like a rabbit. He walks so fast that he gets out of breath and must stop repeatedly to blow. His halts to pant become more frequent and longer, and at the end of the day he may even find, to his chagrin, that some tortoise has arrived ahead of him. The experienced hiker starts more slowly and finishes strong. He may stop often to admire the view, or to take pictures, or to watch an interesting bird, but he travels at a pace such that he seldom needs to blow when hiking on a trail. An exception may be a short stop to rest his shoulders when he has a heavy pack. Even then he seldom removes his pack but merely sits where it is supported by a rock or the slope of the hill.

On the upgrade it is the vertical and not the horizontal distance which counts. This requires that pace be greatly reduced on steep pitches. One need not breathe much harder on a climb than on the level. On a trail one should not cut across switchbacks, partly because it breaks down the side of the trail, making it vulnerable to water erosion, but also because the long way around is equivalent to a lower gear and is more efficient. The principle of steady travel at a comfortable pace is a very important one which comes hard to some eager enthusiasts.

How to walk

Seek a rhythmic stride, however fast or slow. Learn to swing your hips a little to lengthen your stride. People who toe out too much lose some of the spring of the foot as well as the fully effective use of various foot and leg muscles. Cushion the stride with slightly flexed knees. This becomes more important on downgrades, and with a pack. On steep upgrades, plant the feet flat; do not hold the foot up on the toes for this overworks calf muscles and may inflame the heel tendon. If the grade is too steep, zigzag, step a little sideways, or use irregularities of the ground to support the heel in a comfortable high position.

It has been emphasized that pace must be steady, and slow enough to obviate frequent rest periods. On steep ascents a brief pause with each stride, or group of strides, will enable you to avoid breathlessness. It seems awkward at first but becomes second nature with practice. On terrain smooth enough to permit small, equal strides, the pause can come most effectively just as each foot is planted on the ground and before the weight is shifted forward; locking the rear knee rests the leg muscles. Where possible, avoid a very steep line of travel by making short zigzags. Thigh muscles have the best leverage when the knee is not much bent. Where a steep line of travel is necessary, it sometimes is preferable to pause in the middle of each stride as one foot passes the other. On uneven terrain, such as on talus, it is often easier to maintain balance if several quick steps are taken between pauses on rocks suitable to stand on.

Clothing

The body must get rid of the extra heat generated by heavy exercise. There is no more sense in making it difficult than there would be in hindering the passage of air through the radiator of an automobile with a hot engine. It is, therefore, a mistake to wear a heavy woolen shirt or a jacket which is not actually needed for warmth. A hiker will perspire amply for health even though his body remains dry because of low air humidity, and excessive sweating only depletes the body's salt and water stores.

Peel off layers as the sun climbs higher, but avoid another danger. A man with a well-tanned body may hike stripped to the waist, or even in shorts, if there is no brush to scratch his legs, but do not be fooled by a back-yard tan. One should be very cautious till he learns what his body can take at high altitudes where the burning ultra-violet radiation is much stronger than at the seashore. Tanning and burning are different processes; the former builds new tissues in the skin and takes time with repeated judicious exposure; the latter, if it goes as far as blistering, destroys tissues and is an actual setback to tanning. Begin, at least, by wearing a light shirt. A man carrying a pack cannot afford to burn his shoulders!

Thunderstorms are not infrequent in the afternoons in the high mountains, and the temperature can change suddenly from summer to winter. It is wise, therefore, to have readily available, a sweater or jacket, and a light poncho, parka, or other weatherproof covering. When one is traveling with a burro or mule, baggage is roped down tightly under a pack cloth, and therefore, it is convenient to carry maps, lunch, first-aid, and photographic equipment in a small rucksack. As the weather turns cooler, put on wraps *before* you get chilled.

Shoes

The selection of proper shoes is of the utmost importance. Chapter 6, on equipment, will discuss advantages of different types. The footgear should be *well* broken in to the feet *in advance* of the trip. Soften the leather by light waxing and take some hikes near home. This will also help to toughen the feet and foot muscles.

Avoid blisters, for the sake of both yourself and your companions. A person with a badly blistered foot is in worse condition for travel than an automobile with a flat tire; a tire can be changed. A backpack places an extra load upon the feet; make due allowance till you find what they can take.

In chapter 8, you will find information about the treatment of blisters; we emphasize here the following precautions; keep socks free of wrinkles; lace shoes just tightly enough to prevent rubbing—especially on long descents; stop at the slightest suspicion of irritation to investigate, and cover a threatened spot with adhesive; keep the feet clean and dry. If a stream must be forded, take off the socks (shoes may be worn if the feet are tender, or if there is danger of being cut), and put the socks back on after the crossing.

Food and water

The blood in your body can nourish the muscles during exercise, or it can supply the digestive organs for a heavy meal, but it cannot do both effectively at the same time. If you hit the trail promptly after breakfast it is therefore desirable to take it easy the first half hour till the stomach is partly emptied. It is good to take a short siesta after lunch before pushing on. It is a pleasant time of day to bathe, wash socks, or enjoy the sun and be lazy for a few minutes.

Another thing to consider is the digestibility of food in relation to physical exertion. Fat slows digestion and should be avoided at breakfast or lunch on hard days. Protein digests faster but remains in the stomach for some time, which is undesirable before a climb. Carbohydrate digests in the intestine and is the best food to nibble on the trail or use for fuel before a quick start. A readily digestible lunch item consists of one of the dry cereals with milk made from whole milk powder and water, eaten from the tin cup carried on your belt.

The body does not digest any food well when fatigued. At the end of a hard day don't sit right down and gorge yourself. Drink a cup of tea or beef broth, relax for half an hour, and then tie into some solid food with enhanced appetite and improved gastric powers.

It is better to nibble often during the active part of the day than to consume a few large meals. Get into the "morning-brunch, afternoon-snack" habit. Load up in the evening and raid the larder again before hitting the sack if you are still hungry.

Those of you who have learned, on deserts, in jungles, or in the army what it is like to be thirsty are likely to have concluded that it is better to carry a canteen of luke-warm water to the next cool stream than to get into trouble for lack of a drink. However, water is abundant in most of the mountains that are attractive enough to have trails, and therefore seldom needs to be carried. If water is plenti-ful, drink often. If water is scarce, tank up where you can and take it slowly, particularly if it is very cold; you will feel lazy until the water in your stomach reaches body temperature, but it is worth it. You may have to do most of your rehydrating in the evening, with lots of soup and drinks (such as tea and broth) before or during supper, and with a pot of water, tea, hot jello, or lemonade handy at campfire. If snow is eaten to stay thirst, it should be melted in the mouth before it is swallowed. When climb-ing a mountain, stop several hundred feet below the sum-mit, heap your cup with snow, place several small dark rocks on the snow, and place it in the sun, taking care to remember the spot. On the way down you will have a cup of water.

Much salt is lost with perspiration and needs to be replaced if one is to feel fit and to avoid headaches or even sunstroke. Some people add a pinch of salt to each drink of water. Others prefer to season food heavily. Salt pills may be desirable in desert mountains.

Off-trail travel

The backpacker enjoys a certain degree of independence from trails because his equipment is with him and he can camp almost any place. Even burro packers can in some places get off the main trails and enjoy the challenges of picking their own routes and exploring wilder regions. However, off-trail travel calls for some extra experience, caution, and foresight.

The most rewarding cross-country trips are often short excursions or loops taken in forests, along streams, or through meadows. There is no hurry. Itinerary can be changed at any time and a return to base made at will. Even though an excursion from trail or camp is to be short, equipment must be sufficient to make an overnight bivouac bearable and safe, if not comfortable. Consider wraps and extra food.

If the excursion is to be more strenuous or extended, the leader will be responsible for such community equipment as climbing rope, repair kit, and extra first aid. Flashlight and matches are musts. A down sleeping bag per party can be invaluable in case of accident or unexpected delay. The one time the bag of one of us was used at 14,000 feet, near the summit of the North Palisade, justified the many times it was carried up mountains on one-day climbs —often to the amusement of others. A sleeping bag can become the most important item of first-aid equipment.

Most side trips are anchored to a base camp and have an objective, a certain lake or waterfall, or a mountain summit. Be sure that *every* member of your party will be up to the projected trip, and be *sure* that you have competent leadership. Know what you plan to do, don't just strike out to undertake a climb for which you may discover you do not have the strength, equipment, or experience. The novice need not be afraid to explore and learn new tricks, but he should go prepared, and not be too proud or too eager to turn back short of his goal.

Do not underestimate the time your trip will require. Each hiker must learn to gauge the pace he can handle. making allowance for current physical conditions. Until personal experience is acquired, allow one hour per 2½ linear miles and add 1 hour per 1,000 vertical feet when climbing at moderate altitudes and much more at high altitudes or with a heavy pack. A full breath at 11,000 feet draws into your lungs only two thirds as much oxygen as at sea level. A leader must learn the strength of his party and get the knack of judging the difficulty of the terrain from a distance. Never figure too close—it allows you no margin of safety in case of a thunderstorm or sprained ankle.

Route selection

The correct route is all-important. Returning from the summit of Mount Darwin with a mixed party of teen-agers one of us once met two husky-looking young men who had been trying to find a way up for a week. Seek the advice of a man who has made the trip or read about the route if possible. In any event, the leader will select (or identify) the route by study of the map and, if it is to be a climb, particularly by careful inspection of the ground from a distance. At close range it is too late, for one cannot see the route for the rocks. The leader will above all consider the safety of the route. This will concern particularly the upper part of the climb. If you hope to do any real rock work, get some advance practice under the guidance of experienced friends, or at least consult the sections on rock climbing and route selection in the *Manual of Ski Mountaineering* (see bibliography). The technical aspects of route selection therein described are beyond the scope of this book, but above all remember the greatest danger on most climbs is from falling rock. Even a small rock dislodged by one climber can be crippling if it strikes another. Large rocks loosen others and are extremely dangerous. Let no man climb far below another if there is a remote chance that rocks may be dislodged. Pick your route to avoid chutes full of loose rocks or master the technique used by experienced climbers in crossing such places.

If several routes are judged to be safe, it is usually desirable to select the easiest. This is not necessarily the most direct. Look for relatively smooth open ground and plan a steady ascent as gradual as possible and free of ups and downs. Very steep snow banks are dangerous, and you will get your shoes wet in snow after the sun has softened the surface, so avoid at least the big patches. Talus (defined below) may or may not be difficult depending upon the size of the blocks and their stability. Scree is fast going down but exasperating going up. Smooth rock outcrops may be easy if not too steep. Ridges are often easier and usually safer than gullies; they afford two ways out of a bad spot; chutes are often blind alleys.

The detailed route

The leader of a cross-country party must really select two routes, the main route and the detailed route. We have just discussed the first; it is the major plan of progress. The second is the problem of crossing the next 100 yards along the main route with least effort or delay. Should he go around those down trees to the right or left? At what point should he cross that strip of snow? Is there a deer trail through that thicket? Where is the best place to ford the stream ahead? To select the detailed route takes constant attention. The leader must look ahead, not contemplate his feet. His efforts will be rewarded by a saving of effort and by the steady progress of his party.

Talus and scree

The jumbled pile of broken boulders which have come to rest below the bare cliffs on a mountain is called talus. Higher up the rocks are small, in gravel beds called scree.

It is seldom possible to avoid crossing talus slopes on mountain climbs. The novice is nearly halted. The expert seldom slows his pace and often finds talus good fun. Do not climb up over one table-sized block only to slither down into a deep hole and start another difficult scramble up the next boulder. This way your total vertical ascent may be fifty times the net ascent. With a pack, such up and down progress is almost prohibitive. Unless the talus blocks are exceptionally large one can stay on top of the pile. Step or hop from rock to rock selecting the route with care far enough ahead to avoid blind alleys. Play a game with yourself—never make a rock shift under your weight. It takes a careful eye to judge the stability of every rock, and practice to step on possibly loose chunks so that they cannot turn. Move smoothly and steadily so that if a rock should tip under you, you will be away to the next rock and will not be thrown off balance. Use your hands for balance and to steady yourself against a rock in passing, but let your legs do the work.

Scree is almost impossible on the way up but may save time and offer some fun coming down. Run down if you wish but not at top speed and not with big strides. Keep your legs under you as the skier does, and for the same reason—to help you recover from unexpected rough spots.

Do not step on sand or dirt which covers smooth rocks. There is no more certain way to take a spill! A zigzag descent is easier on the legs and safer if you trip—you will not land on your head so far down the mountainside. Take short steps on all rough or loose ground. If you wear gloves when running down scree you may avoid abrading a hand when you use one to make a quick recovery from slipping on a rock concealed by sand.

Snow

Innocent-looking summer snow slopes may be very dangerous. In descending a steep snowbank, one can glissade or slide with the upper foot half a length in advance of the lower, and balancing with the arms. By assuming the sideslipping position of the skier and edging the shoes one can go diagonally and thus control the run. It is important that there be an outrun so that there is no danger of hitting rocks should one fall or lose control.

The rocks at the edge of a snow bank often melt the snow below the surface. One should therefore step onto a snow bank with caution to avoid falling through the crust and possibly wrenching a leg.

Fording streams

If a stream must be crossed, look for a fallen log or a series of steppingstones; if you have a pack, jumping from one slippery rock to another can be dangerous, so don't be afraid to wade with your socks off, but if the bottom is rough, put your shoes on to protect against cuts or bruises of the feet. It takes very tough feet to continue the march in wet socks even for a moderate distance.

If it is necessary to cross a swift stream, carry a pack for weight and select a stout pole to use as the third leg of a tripod on the upstream side. It will increase your stability enormously. If your pack has a waiststrap, untie it, so as to be able to jettison the pack if you should lose your footing.

About being lost

If a person finds that he is lost, he must above all not become panic-stricken but should sit down and take stock, and, ordinarily, stay right where he is till found. If he is likely to have to stay out all night, he should gather a good supply of firewood for warmth and as a beacon to searchers. In open country a flashlight can be seen for miles at night.

There is little excuse for getting lost unless snow or fog make visibility poor. On trails through forested country, blazed trees and the wear of feet and hoofs have made the way plain. It is more difficult to keep oriented off-trail in forested country. Go to high ground for a view of the country if necessary. In open terrain one avoids getting lost by keeping himself constantly posted regarding his whereabouts and by tracing his progress on a good map. In stony country the trail, if any, is marked by "ducks," which are two or more stones piled on top of each other in a way that nature could hardly duplicate. But some of us have learned to be skeptical about ducks we have found off trails on supposed knapsack routes. Few people consider that when they make a ducked trail they are, in effect, saying to those who will follow, "I have scouted this route to the end and know it to be a better route than you could pick. There are good reasons for marking this trail and I will mark it all the way."

4. Camping Technique

SUPPOSE THAT, by following all the prescribed hints and official doctrine, you have been having a good day on the trail. When should you end it?

First, you should stop before you or any other members of the party become too tired. Of course, if you have all set out to cover as much ground as physically possible between sunrise and sunset—which is good, satisfying fun when you are young, and a splendid topic of conversation when you have grown too old to do it any more—you should not heed this advice. Being rested is by no means the only state of enjoyment in the mountains, for surely the harder you pound your feet, the pleasanter will be the stop when it comes.

More important than avoiding a reasonable amount of fatigue is the need to allow plenty of time to make a good installation once the campsite has been chosen. With this in view, the book should say, "Allow two hours of daylight for making camp, preparing dinner, and getting ready to bed down." This is the ideal for comfort.

Some of us, however, don't always like the ideal and the comfortable. Some of us remember clearly that the finest days of all on the trail were those on which we disregarded good judgment and trudged right on past that critical angle of the sun's journey that says "camp now." We trudged right on until the sun was down; we watched the shadows grow longer and the colors grow soft. We were out looking and drinking it in—and not puttering over pots on a smoky fire—when the blue got deep enough, just deep enough, to let the first star come through. We had seen the blaze on the peaks change to a flush, to a steel gray, to a vague shadow before we called it a day. What of it? Our cooking fire still lit; a campfire lit at the same time brought the trees in for a closer look. Water still boiled, food still cooked. And if the cup so shaded the food we were eating that we couldn't see which course was which, we still knew what the food had looked like on earlier days, and it still tasted all right. We all worked a little more purposefully than we did when making early camp. So we hadn't suffered at all up until then, and we remember a distinct advantage when it came to selecting bedsites. It was too dark to see the hummocks and hollows, the rocks and pine cones. All the sites looked good. And we were just tired enough to have them feel good, too.

Having now made it clear that the camping technique we would prescribe is a point of departure and not a long corridor without escape, we list without further qualification the standard procedures for making, using, and breaking camp.

Choice of campsite

Requirements of a site, in order of importance, are:

1) Safety. The site should be free of danger from snow or rock avalanche. Since wind may come up unexpectedly,

care should be taken to see that any dead trees or branches overhead are likely to stay there. Camps in desert climates should avoid the courses of flash floods.

2) Feed. If animals are used, adequate feed and water must be available reasonably near to camp. See chapter 12.

3) Water. The backpacker himself requires very little. Some water-purifying method (Halazone tablets; boiling) should be used unless the stream can reasonably be assumed to be safe. One of the pleasures of the deeper wilderness is that this can usually be taken for granted without undue risk.

4) Wood. Backpackers, being free to camp almost anywhere, would do well to avoid heavily used areas, and will be rewarded by finding firewood more plentiful, and traces of heavy use less plentiful. It is not difficult for a knapsacker to add to his pack enough wood for cooking, thus permitting a camp above timberline. Where ample wood is available it is nice to have a campfire after supper (Indian-like, we prefer sitting close to a small fire rather than far from a blaze—a wood-conserving preference). Resinous woods, especially the pines, make excellent firewood and are easily handled. Dead wood broken off a tree is drier and burns better than sticks picked off the ground. Dry wood can be broken by striking it over a sharp rock; an ax is seldom required for either gathering or cutting firewood.

5) Bedsites. For a comfortable night's rest, each in the party would like a level bedsite, well-drained, and sheltered from wind. A soft covering of duff helps. Sand and meadow are unyielding, although usable; the meadow is usually damp and cold. On a clear night it helps to have foliage between yourself and the absolute zero of interstellar space.

6) Warmth and shelter. Canyon bottoms are the preferred route of most of the cold, hurried air in the region. Prefer benches with some tree screen, and anticipate the winds in the camp layout. The weather otherwise being calm, wind blows up the slope during the day, down at night. Anticipate, too, the course of all temporary streams should it rain—don't have your bedsite in one.

7) Conveniences. If the country abounds in the previously listed assets of a good campsite, then select from these the camp that has (*a*) a large boulder in front of which you can build your campfire and against which you can sit, (*b*) flat rocks for tables and down logs for seats, (*c*) a pool deep enough for swimming or bathing.

8) *Sine qua non*. And though your campsite bestow on you all these things and have no view, it profiteth you nothing.

Making a camp

Once a site has been selected (and members of the party who are off scouting elsewhere have been gathered in), the following order of activity is a good one to follow:

1) Use or reconstruct an old fireplace rather than make a new scar.

2) Get a pot of water, place it on your fireplace before making the finishing touches, and light the fire with whatever squaw wood is within reach. You'll need hot water soon, and it might as well be heating while you are getting things organized.

3) Get the necessary food and utensils hot. Here it helps the cook's disposition if each person knows what he has and where he has packed it. Odds and ends from the packs should not be scattered around.

4) Set up shelter. If tents are pitched, remember the rubber-band ties (see chapter 6) and the tent will be

much more likely to weather a storm or someone's falling on it. If there are guy ropes, hang something white in the middle of each so that they will not become tripwires after dark.

5) Prepare the bedsites (this would precede step 4 for tents with floor). Most woodcraft books recommend a bough bed. This is a holdover from the day when one less tree didn't make any difference. Today most of our wilderness is used so much that every consideration must be given the natural scenery. The cutting or breaking of boughs opens up just that many avenues of infection to the tree, and a pile of dead branches or a dead tree is not going to be very scenic later in the season or in years to come. The pitch would stick to your sleeping bag, and besides, in most regions it is against the law to cut green boughs. There is usually enough duff under a tree (on the upper side if on a hill) for a good bedsite once the cones and rocks have been cleared away. If not, some needles may be borrowed from near-by trees. Yellow pines and white-bark pines make the best needle beds; lodge-pole pines make the worst. A small hollow under the hips adds greatly to comfort. If rocks are lined up around the bedsite to hold the duff together, it is a good thing to scatter them again when you break camp rather than leave them there like tombmarkers.

6) If it is dark, or even just cool, by the time dinner is ready, start the campfire—again in a place where there's already a scar—and eat in comfort. The dishwashers will appreciate it too. Then settle down and really relax around the campfire while you watch the tongues of flame as have countless men before you.

7) Before you leave the fire for bed, see that it is out, and spare yourself the nightmare (real or imaginary) of discovering that a wind has sprung up in the night to

drop glowing embers on your tents and sleeping bags. You need not drown the fire at this time, simply let it burn down and separate all its elements. A piece of wood will not burn for long without moral support from another piece alongside it.

8) Remember the feelings of those who will follow you and make your camp more pleasant for yourselves by concentrating your sanitary facilities in one area, and in a spot that will not likely be used by other campers for any other purpose. Then consider the ways of the cat: dig, and cover—everything. If there are many in the party, improvise a slit trench, partly fill it after each use, and close it when breaking camp.

9) It is assumed that there is an equitable sharing of duties. This is normally true of small parties, but it sometimes happens that if the group exceeds nine or ten, one or two individuals may let their community spirit slide. If dronishness develops, a confidential word from the leader to the offender will usually snap him into cooperating. The man who habitually winds up on a remote rock when dishes are to be washed, or who always manages to appropriate the light and easy items when packing up, had best be left at home next time.

10) Camp should be secured the last thing before retiring. In bear country food can sometimes be tied in a tree, but is usually placed in packs and taken to the bedsites where the bear must waken someone to get at it. The steps to take when so awakened will depend upon the situation and terrain. Bears usually don't like the rattling of pans or a flashlight beam in the eye. Lightweight camp marauders (mice, etc.) can usually be discouraged by placing any tempting morsels in a pot and weighting the lid with rocks. Deer may take any item which is salty. See that camp is wind and waterproofed. Shoes left in the open

should be upside down. Some shoe greases make leather appetizing to certain rodents.

11) Sleeping is usually automatic enough out in the open, but the problem of controlling temperature can interfere with its soundness. If you are traveling as light as possible, you will have a sleeping bag of minimum weight and on a cold night may have to rely on the additional insulation of clothing. If you are cold, you should wear all the clothing you can get on, but it should be perfectly dry and as loose as possible. If the night becomes too warm, your temperature may be progressively reduced by getting the head, shoulders, and arms outside of the bag.

Laying over

A layover day is a good time to check and repair equipment and to turn sleeping bags wrong-side out to air and dry. If camp is to be left for a side trip, fires must be out. Articles left behind should be weatherproofed, no matter how clear the sky in the morning.

It is recommended that occasional layover days be planned simply to take it easy. Find a flat streamside rock. Sun and doze on it; look at the branches against the sky and find out what goes on in a quiet pool. If this is too dull for you, we are sorry. We can only suggest that you might fall back on a book—the kind that doesn't read too swiftly but sends you off on lazy mental side trips at least once every paragraph. If you can't find such a book, you might take along a notebook and write it!

Breaking camp

There is almost nothing quite so gruesome as getting up while it is still dark, but there is, on the other hand, almost nothing quite so rewarding once you have managed to survive the first horrible half hour. Travel in the cool hours is far less taxing than in the heat. On the Sierra Club trips for which that great age range was claimed it is very doubtful if the less rugged members of the party could finish some of the longer moves if they did not start out by dawn. There is an abundant supply of some as-yet-unisolated stimulant in early-morning mountain air. And sun-up is a beautiful time to be looking through that air from high places.

Whether or not you choose to start early and coast through the day, there are a few pointers on cleaning up and packing up to bear in mind:

1) While breakfast is cooking, any garbage, including cans, should be burned. Heat removes the protective coating from the cans and hastens their rusting, simplifies smashing them, and destroys odors which are tempting to bears *et al.* The cans may then be (*a*) placed in a disposal bag if one exists or (*b*) far preferable, be carried away in your own knapsack or kyack back to the road for later disposal. An empty can is lighter than a full one, you are in better condition for being in wilderness when you emptied it, and you *can* take it with you!

2) The fire should be thoroughly drowned. There must be no possibility whatsoever of its reviving, and you must guarantee it. Covering the fire with nonorganic soil, as is frequently recommended, has two disadvantages: (*a*) it is hard to be sure that there is no combustible material mixed with the soil or that a root system will not carry the fire to the surface elsewhere; and (*b*) a dirt-covered fireplace repels the next traveler, who builds another and multiplies the scars.

In packing up, each person should develop a standard procedure so that he can put his load together with a minimum of lost motion. He should remember what he had in his pack when camp was made and, giving thanks for all of it that has been eaten, should pack it again and remember where it is. In most parties, it is a good idea to have a lightweight spring scale along to check loads. It is important to morale that the slower hikers be satisfied that they are not carrying more than their share.

With a last-minute drink of water and a check of the area to see that nothing is forgotten and everything is at least as clean as when the party arrived, the new day's travel is under way.

5. Food and Cooking

THE PROCESS OF TRANSFORMING part of the load on his back into appetizing meals is one of the knapsacker's most pleasurable activities, so much so that failure to plan and to cook the right amount of the right food in the right way can ruin a trip. Fortunately there is some leeway in the interpretation of the word "right." The backpacker needs no wide knowledge of foods and their preparation. Several factors work to the advantage of even the completely novice wilderness cook. First, he exerts himself enough—and his party does too—not to be too demanding about what he eats; certainly he will be more the gourmand than the epicure. Second, few are likely to complain to the cook, out of fear of being handed the stirring spoon. Third, quite often—frequently out of preference—dinner may not be ready until campfire time, when it is too dark to see clearly just what is being eaten. All in all, the novice will get on very well, inventing as he goes, experimenting to see if peanut-butter soup, for example, is really fit to eat, and finding out for certain that an accidental combination of macaroni, cheese, and chocolate is not very fit.

There is always the hard way to learn, of course; this chapter is intended primarily to suggest how the novice may avoid it. The chapter is written without a woman's touch—and shows it. Nor were any 19th-century wilderness cooks consulted on how to live royally off the country on wild berries and grouse. Moreover, those who care so much about cooking that they want to spend most of their time fussing over elaborate dishes already have so many culinary predilections that we'd be wasting our time in trying to add any of ours. This is simply about basic food.

Quantity

Backpacking and burro chasing is work (in the physical sense only, of course) and work requires calories. There are two effective sources of calories on a mountain trip—the food one eats and one's personal reserve of fat. On short trips of a few days even a very large deficiency in food may not be noticed. The few pounds of body weight that will be lost are quickly regained upon return to adequate diet. Consequently there will be varied accounts about how little food some parties have been able to get by on. If, however, a party wishes to maintain body weight and avoid physical deterioration, however imperceptible, a definite minimum amount of food is required. A person of average size, not out to break records in trail or cross-country travel in the mountains—and not trying to break records for loafing either—will use nearly 3,500 calories daily, and can obtain this energy from about 2¼ pounds per man-day of food provided it has very low water content and high calorific value. Practically every group will tend to underfeed itself, however, regardless of how much food is taken along, and most parties don't eat more than

2 pounds per man-day on short trips. This is what usually happens: If the party puts in several strenuous days, its members get too tired to eat enough at dinnertime. They forget to drink enough water during the day and make up for it with watery—and low calorie-value dishes. Unless they eat two lunches a day (a mid-morning brunch and the conventional lunch a little past noon), they eat too little of the rather dry and not too inspiring luncheon menu. Finally, they dash out of the mountains hungry to revel in steaks, milk shakes, and fresh fruit. They probably enjoy themselves, but we maintain that a well-fed party fares better.

Considerations governing the choice of food

Recognizing that each person will take what he likes if he can get it, we go on to suggest:

1) Food should be easily digestible for parts of the trips where meals are to be rushed and followed quickly by exertion.

2) Food should be easy to prepare unless camp cookery is one of the main objects of the trip.

3) Time required for cooking should be short. In mountains remember that higher waters boil cooler. Sea-level cooking time doubles at 5,000 feet elevation.

4) Foods likely to burn or stick to the pot should be frowned upon at the grocer's or they will be at camp later on. In camp the law reads that he who burns the pot also cleans it.

5) Bulky (i.e., space-consuming) foods should be few; a bulky pack is awkward for you to handle and tiring for others to look at.

6) Water should come from the stream, not with the food.

Suitable foods are listed in the Appendix (p. 144). Substitutions may, of course, be made for the specific items on the list, but major changes in the total weight called for in each category might throw the diet out of balance. Neither poor balance nor a vitamin deficiency would be serious on a one- or two-day trip, but on a long trip, one would begin to crave the kinds of food necessary to correct the diet. See the appendix for food lists.

Repacking

Food should be repacked if it is in containers which are breakable, heavy, or hard to pack without wasting space. For most dry foods—flour, sugar, dried fruits, and vegetables—the best container is usually a cloth sack tied at the top. The sacks can be made of any tightly woven cloth, but waterproof material is desirable for carrying items which should be kept free of moisture—salt, sugar, highly desiccated fruits, and powdered milk. Sacks are light and they can be crammed into every corner of your pack. If they are not transparent, a variety of colors will help you identify food when camp is set up.

Cooking equipment

Cooking equipment and the preparation of a fireplace are discussed in chapter 6.

Building fires

If you are a Boy Scout, you are already skilled at lighting a fire in the wind and rain, with no paper, using one match or fewer. If you are not, here are a few simple pointers. Small dead branches are easily broken from trees and are normally drier than wood which is on the ground. Dry wood of fair size can usually be broken by striking it over a rock. There are many techniques for fire building. When it comes to lighting fires without pa-

per, there are two kinds of people: (1) those who indis-
criminately gather a generous handful of twigs, needles.
and dead leaves and, looking nonchalant about it, hold the
handful diagonally over a lighted match until the twigs
ignite; and (2) craftsmen who carefully lay four or five
small, dry, resinous twigs over one another, hold one match
close under a point of intersection until ignition takes
place, add the still-burning match to the pile, and follow
this deftly and almost swiftly with a few more small twigs,
a fairly large one as a *pièce de résistance*, a pause, a few
more successively larger twigs and a confident finale of
fire-sized wood. We have already implied which method
is more satisfying.

Persons uncertain of their choice of method or of their
skill, or who expect to light many fires in the rain, may
want to supplement matches with paper, a candle, or lighter
fluid. Such artificial aids are certainly very efficient, but
they rob the business of all art and ceremony.

Further points: If small twigs are not available, make
shavings with a knife. If you want a big fire for warmth,
make it a separate fire and keep the cooking fire small.
For a hot cooking fire, use small wood and add more while
the flame is hot; to cook slowly, use larger pieces or coals.
For good results you must tend the fire to keep it steady.

Breakfast

What to have for breakfast? If you thought of it the
night before you probably cooked some dried fruit while
you sat around the fire after dinner. If not, you may want
to cook some in the morning, preferably the faster minced
dried apples or apricots, or you may skip the fruit in favor
of an early start. To prepare dried fruit, add water to the
desired amount of fruit and let it simmer until soft. The
amount of water required will vary, so until you find out

how much each fruit takes, put in a little more than enough to cover the fruit, and add more as the fruit swells. You are less likely to burn the pot if you add no sugar until you are nearly ready to stop boiling the fruit.

Coffee drinkers usually have pretty definite ideas about how to prepare their morning beverage. In the absence of the usual utensils, you can make passable coffee by dumping about one rounded tablespoon of coffee per cup into boiling water and taking it off the fire as soon as it looks opaque enough. Soluble coffee is far simpler to make and lighter to carry.

To make cocoa, put the required amount of cold water in a pot; add, while cold, enough powdered milk to make full-strength milk. For a smooth mixture, warm the water very slightly as the powder is beaten in with a small wire beater or egg beater. Mix the necessary dry cocoa and sugar and dump the mixture slowly into the milk when hot, stirring briskly. Then bring nearly to a boil and serve. The amount and proportion of cocoa and sugar varies widely with individual taste. For a starter try a generous teaspoon of each per cup of milk, and then adjust to taste when you see what has resulted.

The remainder of your breakfast can be one or more of the following:

1) Dry cereal (most knapsackers will be partial to the only concentrated one—grape nuts) with milk.

2) Cooked cereal (e.g., oatmeal, corn meal, wheat hearts). These are all cooked by pouring the cereal slowly into the correct amount of boiling salted water on the fire, stirring as you pour and as often as needed to prevent sticking and burning, until it tastes cooked. The quantities required vary greatly with the cereal, but until you find out, try ¼ teaspoon of salt, ⅓ cup of cereal, and ¾ cup of water per person, adding more water during cooking

if it gets too thick. The thicker it is the harder it will be to clean the pot. Boil over a slow fire. If you like raisins, date flakes, or apple nuggets with your cereal, give them a head start in the boiling water (but check first to see if others in the party can abide the combination).

3) Hot cakes. If you brought pancake flour you need merely stir in enough water or milk, a little at a time, to produce a medium batter. If you are mixing your own, the mix should include for each man ⅓ cup flour, 1 tablespoon milk powder, 1 teaspoon egg powder (if you have it), ⅙ teaspoon salt, ½ teaspoon baking powder, and ½ tablespoon melted butter or other cooking fat. The flavor can be varied by substituting whole wheat flour or corn meal for about ⅓ of the flour, or by replacing half the flour with cooked rice left over from the night before. It will take nearly a cup of cooked rice to substitute for ⅓ cup of flour.

For cooking hot cakes, the frying pan or aluminum plate must be clean, and well greased with butter or other cooking fat. The fire must be kept steady and low, so that the cakes become golden brown just as they are cooked through but before they dry out.

For syrup, just boil two parts of sugar or brown sugar to one of water. If you want to be deluxe, bring along maple flavoring and use a few drops per batch of syrup.

4) Canadian bacon, ham, spam, etc. These meats can either be fried over a slow fire or diced and boiled with the cereal. Canadian bacon is normally better than ordinary bacon because the latter contains so much fat that most of it is usually wasted.

Lunch

It is not often worth while to cook hot food for lunch, unless it happens to be a very cold day, in which case you might want a hot drink—cocoa, coffee, soup, tea, or jello. If it is not cold, but you don't want to take all your liquid as pure water, you can mix up some milk or make some synthetic lemonade. You can mix up lemon or orange powder such as that supplied in Army C, K, and 5-in-1 rations, or dissolve several pinches of citric acid in a cup of cold water. Add sugar to taste and a crushed vitamin C tablet if desired.

The rest of the meal can consist of cold cereal, pilot bread, pumpernickel or hard crackers with butter, peanut butter or jam; cheese; salami or other luncheon meats; salted nuts, dried fruit, candy, cookies, etc. Fresh-caught mountain trout may be freely substituted if available.

Dinner

For the liquid in it and for its ease of digestion after a hard day, soup makes an excellent first course for dinner—provided that it precedes the main meal long enough not to interfere with eating a full quota of dinnertime calories. To give the soup body it should have ingredients such as one or more of the following: powdered milk, pea flour, soy bean flour, white flour, precooked, dried, mashed potato, or a commercial dried soup stock. Powdered milk dissolves best in lukewarm water, whereas any kind of flour can best be dissolved by first adding water slowly to the flour until a thin batter is obtained and then adding the batter to the soup. Vary the amount of flour to suit your taste, but you can try a rounded tablespoonful per cup of soup. To give the soup flavor it is desirable to include, among other things, some of the following: tomato paste (a 6 oz. can for six to twelve servings), bouillon paste or cubes, dried onion, garlic powder, chili powder, onion powder or salt, celery salt, butter, bacon fat, salt, etc. Most people are surprised to find that they like peanut-butter

soup; this is made by stirring water slowly into peanut butter to produce a thin cream which is added to milk and
flavored with salt and preferably also a little onion. If a
soup has body and an adequately strong flavor, you can
add anything else that strikes your fancy.

Unless you wish to fry some trout, ham, Canadian bacon, or precooked diced potatoes, you will find it simplest
and quite satisfactory to cook only one dish for the main
course of your dinner. If you have been able to purchase
suitable dried vegetables, however, you may wish to cook
them separately.

Macaroni, spaghetti, and noodles are cooked by boiling ten or fifteen minutes in salted water. You can tell
by taste when they are done. Before serving, you should
pour off most of the excess water and stir in a suitable
tasty addition—a liberal amount of grated cheese (about
a cupful of mild yellow cheese for four to six servings) and
some tomato paste, or dried chipped beef and some onion-
flavored cream sauce. The chipped beef may be salty
enough to take care of the paste and water too. For a cup
of cream sauce start with two tablespoons of flour, add
milk slowly until a thin batter is formed, then add the
rest of the cup of milk, and butter, bacon grease, onion salt,
egg powder, or other flavoring; cook slowly while stirring
until thickened, and add to the macaroni.

Rice can be cooked and flavored the same way as spaghetti. It can be cooked quickly if the commercially available precooked rice is used. Otherwise, it takes 30 to 60
minutes to cook, depending on the altitude, and it takes
more water and requires more attention to prevent burning. The time required to cook the starch in the rice can
be reduced by heating dry rice to 250 to 300° F. before
adding water. This can either be done in your oven at
home before the trip, or in a dry pot on your grate (be

careful not to burn it). It will still be necessary, however, either to boil it for some time, or to presoak it in warm water in order to get the kernels soft.

The above starches, particularly rice, are also good eaten with, or mixed with fish. Rice is good with butter, sugar, and cinnamon.

Dried vegetables vary too much to discuss in generalities. Most of them should merely be boiled in salted water an adequate length of time. For many of them, however, no length of time seems adequate. Try them out at home ahead of time, remembering that cooking time increases and willingness to spend it decreases with the altitude. Precooked, diced, or shredded vegetables are likely to cook best. Dried, precooked, powdered or shredded potatoes are easy and quick to prepare and serve with butter, salt, and milk.

If you want your meat separate, you can fry the Canadian bacon, spam, or corned beef, etc., or stir dried chipped beef into a cream sauce, such as described for macaroni. To fry trout you must grease the plate or frying pan well with butter or bacon fat.

For dessert one can have stewed fruit, candy, cookies, jello (preferably with cooked fruit added), or a prefabricated pudding—the kind you simply add hot water to.

Dishwashing

The chief disadvantage of cooking is the resulting array of dirty pots, spoons, and cups which someone (other than the cook) must clean. As soon as a pot is emptied, rinse it out, fill it with water, and put it back on the fire. Do the same with the second pot, and the dish water will be ready when the meal is over. A small amount of detergent will combat grease. A metal woven pot cleaner of some kind of steel wool is helpful in removing the baked food that accumulates near the top of the pot. In a pinch you can do a good job with some sandy moss roots from the stream. It won't hurt to boil any interchangeable eating utensils.

We hope that no one camped upstream from you throws his dishwater back into the stream. The days are gone, now, when there were so few people in the wilderness that such practices didn't matter.

It's worth the extra effort to do an especially good job of cleaning utensils after the last meal of the trip; a light coating of grease will help preserve rustable utensils. The extra effort pays off when the next trip rolls around. And there will have to be more trips.

6. Equipment

A PAINFUL SIGHT for an old-time backpacker is to see a group of tenderfeet full of enthusiasm and expectation of a joyful vacation but loaded down with burdensome and inadequate equipment—tents of canvas which should be carried on a mule, long raincoats which are not only heavy but interfere with hiking, sleeping bags which look like a rolled mattress, pots, pans, and cans which should never have gotten beyond road's end, and packs—everything from a rope suspending an unshapely and weighty mass of camping gear to huge heavy packboards that appear to have seriously depleted the national lumber supply.

For all its bulk and weight the beginner's pack is often without items of equipment which might be required for his safety or comfort; yet it usually contains pieces of bedding, clothing, mess gear, and just plain gadgets for which he will have no need. Sporting goods stores are full of paraphernalia which are excellent for auto camping but entirely out of place on remote trails. Well-intentioned but uninformed salesmen urge all manner of superfluous equipment upon the unsuspecting neophyte.

The old-time backpacker, after meeting such a party, thinks of his own pack in contrast: sleeping bag when rolled not much larger than a metropolitan Sunday newspaper, poncho weighing less than 2 pounds to serve as both tent and raincoat, lightweight nesting mess gear, about 2 pounds of food per day in compact waterproof bags, and so on through the list. He has everything which is essential, but every item is carefully selected for lightness, compactness and adequacy. He will be safe and comfortable come what may, yet his pack is so light and well-designed that he may not bother to take it off when fishing or photographing.

The needs of a backpacker are few; a comfortable pack, protection from rain, clothing and sleeping bag to insure warmth, and finally enough grub to satisfy a mountain appetite. Remaining needs are incidental.

The difference between the old-timer and the tenderfoot does not lie in experience alone. It is to be found also in a difference in attitude. The old-timer does not select his equipment and gear on the basis of its interesting appearance or the recommendation of a salesman or friend. He considers carefully what function each item is required to perform and checks off these functions against the piece of equipment selected. He also considers the climate and terrain where he intends to do his backpacking. If he anticipates only light frost on his trip he does not select an arctic sleeping bag designed for forty below zero. If only occasional rains are to be expected he makes a lightweight poncho serve for both raincoat and tent. Always he insists that every item shall be adequate, light, and compact. Above all he is a modernist claiming for his own pleasure the latest discoveries and technological developments of industry wherever they may help him. What was good enough for father is not good enough for him.

Let us apply this attitude to the selection of specific pieces of backpacking equipment. It must be remembered that every selection involves an individual choice. Some persons are warmer blooded than others, some would rather add a few pounds for complete comfort than go quite so light. And above all, there are many variations of climate and terrain in the mountain regions of the United States. The purpose of this chapter is not to state what is best but how to select the best. A few notes on the use of equipment will be added.

Sleeping bags

Body heat is lost during sleep by: respiration; conduction through the insulating material of which the bag is composed and thence by radiation and conduction from the exterior of the bag; ventilation taking place when warm air leaks out of the bag either through the fabric or through openings; heat of evaporation from the insensible perspiration of the body, between a pint to a quart of water being lost in this manner each night; and radiation and convection from exposed portions of the body. No practical means of minimizing heat losses from respiration and insensible perspiration have yet been developed.

Thermal insulation is directly proportional to thickness of trapped air and independent of weight. Goose and duck down have more bulk for unit of weight than any other material which is usable and available. A mixture of down with 60 per cent small duck (not chicken) feathers is 80 per cent as efficient as pure down but less expensive.

If the inner and outer fabric layers of the bag are stitched together without separating baffles, the sleeping bag is reduced to a series of alternating strips of good and poor insulation, and its thermal efficiency is greatly impaired. This objection is overcome by either (1) an intermediate layer of fabric alternately sewed to the inner and outer fabric layers or (2) narrow strips of cloth sewed to the inner and outer layers of fabric giving approximately a ¾ inch thickness at the seams. Both methods are satisfactory.

Warmth is dependent upon design as well as upon insulating material. To obtain adequate warmth with minimum weight the bag should be as small and as form-fitting as is consistent with comfort but not so small that the outer fabric layer is under tension with resulting compression of the down. In an ideal sleeping bag the outer layer of fabric is sufficiently larger than the inner layer to prevent this.

The design also should have no openings which cannot be adequately closed to prevent loss of warm air from inside the bag. Zippers give better closure than snaps or buttons.

The design of the bag should allow the head and neck to be covered. Experiments have shown that heat loss if these parts of the body are outside the bag can amount to one-quarter of the total heat loss of the entire body.

Tightly woven fabric is necessary not only for downproofness but also to prevent air permeation. Fabric must be of minimum weight consistent with durability. Even in a well-designed bag the fabric weighs more than the filler which provides the warmth. Lightweight, closely woven balloon cloth weighing 2 ounces per square yard will last for years with care. Such a fabric has a tensile strength of 40 pounds per inch. Four ounces per yard should be considered a maximum weight.

Compactness. In backpacking, bulk is almost as important as weight. No bag filler compares with pure down in compressibility. Small duck feathers are only half as good.

Water repellency. Although the backpacker's camping gear will include some sort of rain protection, it is desirable that the exterior of the sleeping bag be water-repellent. Wetting may come from unexpected showers or contact with damp ground or the wet interior of a tent. The bag should not be waterproof since this will make drying the

filler difficult and will condense the insensible perspiration given off by the body at night.

It should be noted that a waterproof fabric is either
coated or impregnated with plastic, oil, or wax so as to
form an impermeable film. The fabric serves only as struc-
tural reinforcing of the film. Such a fabric will "sweat,"
that is, condense moisture, on the interior unless a free
flow of air is provided. This makes it useless for sleeping
bags and tight-fitting garments but useful for ponchos and
tents, where a free flow of air can be obtained.

Water-repellent fabrics, on the other hand, are treated
with only enough wax or other water-repellent material to
overcome the natural water absorption of the fibers. The
best water repellents are of the permanent type, of which
Zelan is the best known. These will remain through several
launderings or dry cleanings. Such fabrics, even though
tightly woven, permit the passage of evaporated moisture
through them. Tightly woven, water-repellent fabrics are,
therefore, largely wind-tight, but are permeable to moisture. One of the best water-repellent fabrics developed in
recent years is the so-called "Shirley Cloth," named for the
British laboratories which conceived it. The yarns of this
fabric are only slightly twisted. When such a cloth is wet
the swelling cotton yarns conform to and plug up the small
holes in the cloth. Treatment with water repellent gives
further protection. The army has standardized this cloth
as "Oxford wind-resistant cloth" in various weights for
rain-resistant clothing, sleeping-bag covers, and lightweight tents. Information about availability of fabrics can
be obtained from the "Equipment Bulletin" (see p. 149).

The backpacker has a choice of two methods for making
his sleeping bag water repellent.

1) He may use a separate water-repellent outer cover.
This design was adopted by the U.S. Army to permit the

use of one cover for blanket bags, single down bags (mountain), and double down bags (Arctic). Two water-repellent fabric layers protect the filling of the bag, permitting it to be exposed to heavy rains without soaking.

2) Or for the outer surface of the sleeping-bag he may use a water-repellent Shirley-type fabric. This alternate saves about two pounds and substantially reduces bulk. It is the better selection for summer use in all but the rainiest regions.

Comfort. A prevailing but mistaken notion exists that a sleeping bag must be large to be comfortable. This is probably the explanation for the public acceptance of large rectangular bags which only require the addition of bedposts for conversion into a standard bed. A sleeping bag is not a bed but an article of clothing designed for sleeping. Like clothing, it should shift and rotate with the occupant. It takes a few nights for campers to adjust themselves to the use of form-fitting bags, but almost invariably thereafter they prefer them.

Obviously, the bag should not be a strait jacket. It must allow adequate room for moving the arms into various sleeping positions. Experience has shown that maximum warmth and comfort and minimum weight is secured in bags which are widest at the elbows and taper toward each end.

Married couples often use double bags, i.e., bags big enough for two. Owing to the reduction in total outside bag area, a double bag need only be three quarters or less of the weight of two single bags to provide the same warmth.

Recommendations. The ideal sleeping bag for the backpacker for mountain summer use (occasional rain, temperatures not below 15° F.) should meet the following specifications.

1) Its design should be form-fitting, similar to the U.S. Army mountain bag.

2) The filler should be of 2 pounds of 100 per cent duck or goose down.

3) The interior fabric should be 2-ounce nylon. Nylon's extreme smoothness adds to comfort, its abrasion and "sweat rot" resistance add to its life.

4) The exterior fabric should be 3–4-ounce cotton, Oxford-weave Shirley-type, treated with permanent water repellent.

The nearest approach to the ideal bag presently available are the Army mountain bag, the inner bag of the Army Arctic bag, and copies of these produced by a few manufacturers. For those who wish to make their own bags, the design can be obtained from the Office of the Quartermaster General, Washington, D.C. The item is "Bag Sleeping Mountain" in army nomenclature.

In warm regions, where minimum temperatures as high as 50° F. are expected, a blanket, the fuzzier the better, can be sewed into a form fitting shape (Army specification: "Bag Sleeping Wool"). Either a water-repellent shell or a poncho should be used around the blanket bag for rain protection and additional warmth.

Notes on use. Before using, shake the bag well from each end toward the middle. Warmth depends on fluffiness.

Dry the bag frequently, exposing both interior and exterior. Down and fabric absorb considerable moisture without showing dampness. Thorough drying increases the fluffiness of the down.

If the bag is too warm, sleep with head out and open the zipper of the bag. If necessary, sleep with arms and shoulders out. The body is an efficient circulating heating system and can be cooled by partial exposure.

If the bag is too cold, be sure it is adequately fluffed and you are thoroughly closed in from head to foot. Dry clothes loosened but worn also add to warmth. If the ground is cold or too hard for comfort (as it usually is) make a bed of needles, or dry grass. Down is a poor insulator when compressed by the weight of the human body.

A hollow under the hips may increase comfort.

Mattress

Most experienced backpackers prefer to save the weight of a mattress and rely either on their own ability to sleep on the ground or take time to gather the necessary materials for a mattress of twigs, needles, or dry grass.

If, however, glacier or snow camping is anticipated, a mattress is worth carrying. To achieve maximum lightness, minimum storage bulk, and adequate comfort, it should be

1) An air mattress of the air-inflation type. The inflation opening should be large, not like an auto tire valve.

2) Only long and wide enough to extend from shoulders to hips inclusive; 18 x 36 inches is about right. (The packframe or rucksack will hold the feet off the snow, and food bags make a satisfactory pillow.)

3) Not over 3 pounds in weight.

Various small air mattresses are commercially available. The best is a type developed but never mass produced by the Army. It is formed of nylon fabric holding four separate longitudinal plastic tubes. Each tube is individually inflated. Full inflation of outer tubes forms a trough for the body and discourages rolling off during the night.

Raingear

Except for areas free of rain in summer, rain protection must be provided for trail and camp. A wide latitude of

choice exists. The backpacker must consider several factors. If expected rains are warm and infrequent, only the
minimum protection is necessary and some hardy souls
will be willing to get wet and rely on overhanging rocks
or a brush shelter for protection and a blazing fire for drying. If expected rains are cold and wind-driven and likely
to continue for several days at a time, most backpackers
will prefer to carry a thoroughly rainproof tent. Bearing
in mind the variations in climate under which raingear is
to be used, as well as your personal predelictions, base
your selection upon considerations of weight, storage bulk,
wear resistance, tear and tensile strength, resistance to
water penetration, condensation of moisture, weight when
wet, and adequacy of design.

Fabric. The choice is narrowed to two types of fabrics,
both of which have their advantages and disadvantages,
and accordingly their proponents and opponents. These
fabrics are plastic-coated nylon and lightweight Shirley-
type Oxford. Coated nylon is lighter in weight. Both are
satisfactory in wear-and-tear resistance and tensile strength
if used with reasonable care. Coated nylon is waterproof
but condenses perspiration unless well ventilated. Shirley
cloth will wet through after a few hours when subjected to
rubbing (as when used for a garment) but transmits moisture under drying conditions. Coated nylon dries more
rapidly. Water absorption and resultant weight increase
when wet is less for coated nylon than for Shirley cloth.

Recommendation. Unless long-continued heavy rains
are expected, or unless the camping trip includes the probability of heavy wind-driven rain or snow without forest
or other wind protection, satisfactory rain protection with
least weight and bulk can be secured by use of a coated
nylon poncho, coupled with a lightweight windbreaker
jacket of Shirley cloth. The jacket will be discussed under

"Clothing." The most thoroughly tested poncho design is that adopted by the U.S. Army. Such a poncho is used in several ways:

1) In heavy rain it is thrown over both the hiker and his pack, giving protection to both. Its fullness provides for adequate ventilation and minimizes sweating. It is awkward for climbing over rocks but the edges can be tied around the waist if necessary.

2) When the ground is wet but no rain shelter is necessary it is used as a ground cloth.

3) It can serve as a sleeping bag cover to break the wind or provide hasty rain protection.

4) It can be improvised into an open-end pup tent or a lean-to for rain protection. Several ponchos can be snapped together for this purpose provided they are of the same design.

If climatic conditions require a tent, the tapered tent (see p. 56) is recommended for two or three persons. It can be constructed of either coated nylon or Shirley cloth. Suggested dimensions (in inches) are as follows: width at front, 64, at back 30; height at front 51, at back 20; length of ridge, 88; triangular front flaps, 60 x 60 x 30, joined by 42-inch zipper; width of sod cloths, 10. The Army mountain tent of coated nylon as well as many special designs put out by sporting goods stores are commercially available. Even the lightest are heavy compared with the nylon poncho.

Notes on pitching tents

Tent pegs are not necessary. In forested country they can be made as needed; above timberline rocks can be used to anchor the lines.

The elastic method of pitching tent or poncho prevents tearing and keeps it continuously taut. Rubber bands one

inch wide are cut from inner tubes and tied to all suspension and tension points on the tent or poncho.

If the poncho is pitched as an open-end pup tent strong
cord (about $\frac{3}{16}$ inches in diameter) should be used as a
ridge line, thus taking the strain off the lightweight fabric.

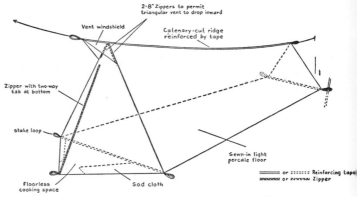

Tapered tent for three men. From *Manual of Ski Mountaineering.*

If the tent is provided with a floor, beds of forest duff
should be placed under (not on) the floor cloth.

Cord for guy lines should not be forgotten. A cinch knot
or hitch should be used that will permit tightening and
loosening of guy lines without the necessity of untying
and retying knots. The rolling hitch can be slipped in any
direction but it tightens under tension.

Clothing

For summer camping in ordinary mountain climates
(occasional rain, temperatures down to light frost) clothing presents no problems—except that most backpackers
carry too much.

Change of clothing. Normally a backpack trip will not last for more than two weeks without a return to base or to a previously established camp. For this reason a change of clothing, except for socks, is unnecessary. Those with strong instincts for cleanliness can take time on a warm day for general laundering operations. Others become oblivious to the problem of clean clothes.

Headgear. A hat should have a brim wide enough to afford sun and rain protection; it should be reasonably waterproof, and flexibility is to be preferred. An old felt hat does the job nicely; so does a cloth hat if constructed of water-repellent fabric.

Underclothes. Most hikers prefer to wear shorts only, without undershirt. Personal preference should govern.

Shirt. A tough shirt is needed. It may be of cotton for warmer climates, wool for cold and rainy areas. One shirt is enough, but a second one is justified if both are to be worn at once for cold weather.

Trousers. Water-repellent twill or Shirley cloth trousers insure reasonable dryness. A 9-ounce fabric should be the top weight limit. Heavier fabrics are stiff, hot, and uncomfortable (duck-hunting trousers are in this class).

Preshrunk blue jeans are satisfactory for mild-weather regions. Cut off the cuffs and collect less dirt.

The U.S. Army mountain pants are hard to beat. They are tough but not too heavy; they are of a roomy, nonconfining cut; there is plenty of pocket space; and, because of their ski-pant treatment at the ankle, they are closed at the bottom and keep the legs amazingly clean in country that is dusty. Hiking shorts—swimming-trunk type—will provide a welcome and cooler variation on sunny days, as well as expediting the tan that most travelers of the trail enjoy collecting. In brushy country the shorts will be worn more comfortably in the rucksack.

Shoes. The kind of shoes to select depends in part upon the nature of the terrain to be traveled. If there is little or no steep snow to travel over, or if the underfooting is for the most part dry and not covered by the acre with baseball-sized sharp rocks, ankle-high sneakers serve admirably. They are very light, inexpensive, and sure-footed. They are not good for a man with weak arches, however, and the canvas tops do not remain intact for more than 100 miles of reasonably rough going. They will wet through very quickly, moreover, and cause foot perspiration to accumulate. Nevertheless, hundreds of hikers have used them happily on month-long Sierra trips. Leather-topped basketball shoes give more support and are much longer-lasting and correspondingly more expensive.

The army's Munson Last, as represented in the G.I. service shoe (or cut-down combat boot), combined with composition soles, is hard to beat for comfort and traction on the summer trail. And if one is packing animals, a leather shoe offers more protection from a hoof. They keep the feet much cleaner than sneakers.

Boots nailed with hob slivers, Swiss edge nails, or Tricounis have a distinct advantage if there is much snow to cover, or in mossy country with a wet summer climate. But nails require more skillful use on rock—especially smooth rock—than does rubber. The best compromise so far discovered for summer mountaineering is the Bramani-type sole, consisting of long-wearing rubber cleats, mounted on a lightweight boot; that is, on a boot much lighter than the army's mountain boot. The Bramani sole holds very well on rock, on snow that is not too hard-frozen and smooth, on glacial ice, on muddy or grassy slopes, and will even do reasonably well, because of the cleats, on wet, mossy rock—but not on smooth wet rock.

A plain leather sole offers so little traction that it is

dangerous in most terrain, and should therefore be avoided.

High boots are usually unnecessary, are needlessly heavy, and restrict the circulation. Trousers of tough material protect the legs sufficiently from brush; and rattlesnakes, if they strike at all, seldom hit above the ankle.

Rubber-cleated (Bramani-type sole) ski boot

Tricouni nail pattern using the heel plate, studs, and edge nails; sponge-rubber heel

Shoes should be fitted to allow plenty of toe room over two suitable pairs of socks. Allow for the tendency for feet to spread under a pack load, but don't have a sloppy fit in the heel. If you put into use shoes which have been in storage for several seasons examine the stitching to be sure that it has not deteriorated. Dress leather shoes lightly with a boot wax to keep them pliable, but do not soften them with too frequent applications of shoe creams or oils.

The necessity for breaking shoes in before the start of a trip is mentioned in several other places in the book, but is again stressed here because of its importance.

Socks. The foot should be well cushioned by two pairs of socks unless experience and good condition prove that one is enough. The inner pair should be smooth and lighter, the outer one of heavy, soft wool. At least one change of socks should be carried. Socks are subject to heavy wear. Only new socks should be taken.

Jacket and sweater. A light windproof-water repellent jacket with hood is very desirable. A sweater will be required in cold regions; where weather is mild a sleeveless slip-on may be adequate.

The pack

The downfall of most amateur backpackers is either a poor pack or lack of knowledge of how to use it. Consideration of the functional requirements of a good pack is necessary.

The combined mass of the pack and the body above the hip should balance on the hip joints with minimum forward lean of the torso. This requirement may sound technical, but is quite simple once it is fully visualized. A hiker compensates for the backward pull of his pack by leaning forward; the greater the backward pull the more he leans to get the body and pack in balance on the hip joints. It is not possible to hike in any other way, and it is not comfortable to hike under a severe forward lean. The practical application of this principle are known to all backpackers.

Heavy articles should be placed as far forward (close

to the back) as possible, either immediately against the pack frame or in the two forward bulges of the rucksack. Heavy articles should also be packed as high as is possible without making the pack topheavy. The reason behind this rule is that a forward lean of the torso (10 degrees for instance) will result in a greater forward movement of the center of gravity of the pack if heavy articles are packed high.

Most of the weight of the pack should rest on the hips. The function of shoulder straps is primarily to hold the pack in position. The pelvic and leg bones with their large muscles are better designed for supporting a load than are the spine and shoulders.

Some sort of a frame is indispensable to transmit the load from the top of the pack to the hips. This in practice is done by (1) the packboard, (2) the Bergans-type rucksack, or (3) two thrust bars connecting the upper point of attachment of the shoulder straps with the lower forward corners of the pack. A belly band at belt height forces the weight into the hips and permits loosening of the shoulder straps.

To compress the pack and concentrate the weight forward, rugged cinch straps or cords are necessary.

A bag with exterior pockets is easier to pack, more waterproof and provides better accessibility than a roll.

Shoulder straps should rest close to the neck. They are uncomfortable, tiresome, and prevent free swinging of the shoulders when they rest near the shoulder tips. This result is secured in all good packs by attaching the shoulder straps close together on the upper portion of the pack.

Shoulder straps should be tapered so as to be broad over the shoulders but narrow under the armpits. Narrow straps of uniform width cut the shoulders; wide straps chafe the armpits.

The bottom attachment of the shoulder straps should be as far back on the pack as practicable. Otherwise the pack is pushed away from the shoulders. This is particularly important with the Bergans-type rucksack, on which shoulder straps should be attached well back of the forward points of the frame.

Recommendation. For loads under 45 pounds the rucksack with either a rigid frame or two thrust bars is generally preferred to the packboard. It must, however, be properly packed with heavy articles forward and high and the rear hump thoroughly compressed. The ideal is a pack that is wide, high and thin when all gear is stowed. The U.S. Army rucksack is of the rigid-frame type. It is satisfactory in design but could be lightened considerably (the Air Corps was getting most of the aluminum when the rucksacks were manufactured). It is too large for most women.

For those who wish to carry heavy loads the pack frame is satisfactory. It may be constructed of aluminum tubing and covered with canvas. For ruggedness and reasonable weight the army plywood pack frame is first choice in this class.

Considerable weight can be saved and the necessity of bending the rucksack frame to fit the user avoided by the insertion in any well constructed rucksack (without frame) of two duralumin bars $\frac{3}{4}$ x $\frac{3}{16}$ x 20 inches. The upper ends of the bars are attached to the shoulder-strap suspension in such manner as to permit free pivoting action. The lower ends of the bars are attached to the lower front corners of the rucksack. A triangle without a bottom member results. The bars are bent and twisted to clear the shoulder blades and held in position on the front surface of the pack by sewing on covering fabric strips. The exact method of attachment of the bars will depend on the construction of the rucksack and the ingenuity of the maker.

Miscellany

Flashlight. Each person should carry a small flashlight (preferably one using a single standard-size cell). It is handy at night. One standard size flashlight for the party (3-cell head-attachment type preferred) is desirable if night travel is expected. The safety value of a flashlight on off-trail travel, and its use in the event one becomes lost are mentioned elsewhere in this book.

Toilet articles. These should be confined to necessaries. Omit the large bath towel. A single light plastic (rayon) towel will suffice. A small sized bar of soap in all probability is more than the party will use—shaving included. If shaving should be deemed a must, one razor will certainly do a party unless all men must shave simultaneously.

Handkerchiefs. Two large bandannas are recommended. Disposable tissues are too bulky, and bulk can be almost as troublesome as weight. (If this counsel is disregarded, disposable tissues should at least be disposed of in the campfire.) Bandannas can also be put over the head to discourage mosquitoes and help keep one's neck warm when it is cold.

Dark glasses. These will be desirable if the trip includes snow, glaciers, or extensive hiking above timberline. If much snow is expected an extra pair of dark glasses for the party should be taken in case there is breakage.

Knife. The new boy-scout-type knife based on the Army and Marine pocket knife is best. A hunting knife is not necessary but one in the party may prove useful in cooking. Hatchets and axes should be left at the roadhead; they are not needed for securing fire wood.

First aid. See chapter 8, Mountain Medicine.

Mess gear. One dessert spoon per person and a pocket knife complete necessary eating tools. A large cup serves as both cup and plate.

Cooking equipment. A gasoline stove is not necessary unless camps above timberline are planned. (For a few such camps wood can be carried.) The primus type is good. The obsolete U.S. Army single burner stove (Coleman type) is efficient but lacks stability, lightness, and compactness. Far superior is the standard Army one-burner stove (Aladdin type). It is designed to fit into the mountain cook set and burns either ethyl or white gasoline. Gasoline requirements can be held to a $\frac{1}{4}$ pint per man day, but don't count on this until you try it. Ordinarily, the camper can find enough dead wood for his fire.

In country where rocks are scarce or are too rounded, pots can be hung over the fire on forked green sticks which have been driven into the ground. If there is an abundance of flat or nearly flat rocks, it is a simple matter to improvise a rock stove. Where convenient it can be built against a large sheltering boulder. There are only two essential features of the stove; it must support two sides of each pot high enough off the ground to permit building a fire underneath, and it must permit adequate flow of air to the fire. The camper can use his ingenuity to get an optimum working arrangement and minimum smoke in the cook's eyes. If the firebox is too deep, more wood is used than need be; if it is too wide, stability of the stove is likely to suffer—the soup likewise.

This sort of open fireplace blackens the kettles, but only to make them more efficient as heat absorbers; a few odd pieces of cardboard between the nesting pots will minimize the spreading of soot, and a bag can be provided to wrap around the outside of the nest to keep the pack clean. A further advantage of the rock stove is that it is thermostatically controlled: if the fire becomes too hot and the pots boil over, the crisis is self-cured. This may seem a very simple observation, but it is surprising how many cooks have been singed a bit while trying to rescue boiling pots that can take care of themselves.

If one cannot be reasonably sure of finding flat rocks, a stiff wire grill, with or without legs, is usually worth its weight. Whenever one can count on the availability of rocks to prop up the corners, an aluminum plate grill is excellent. The plate should be roughly 18 inches by 9 inches by $5/32$ inches thick, with about $1/2$ inch around the edge bent up 30 degrees or so to provide rigidity. If the size is appreciably increased, the thickness must also be increased. The plate is a little heavy (3 lbs.) for a party of two backpackers, but will do for four to six, and serves as a frying pan for hot cakes, sliced meat or fish, as well as for a pot support. In the latter capacity it has the advantage over a wire grill in that the pots don't get sooted, except lightly on the sides. The pots will not heat so fast, however (or burn so fast), as on a direct flame. If the plate gets bent, it is easy to bend it straight again. A hot fire burns the top of the plate clean, and the loose soot can be quickly removed from the bottom by rubbing sand over it with a clump of grass or the sole of one's shoe. Avoid scratching the upper surface. The plate is slipped into a cloth sack and carried in a pack against the pack frame.

Two to four pots are desirable, plus a medium-sized light frying pan if you have omitted the aluminum plate. Usually only two will be on the fire at once, but a third is very convenient for water supply, and a fourth is useful when the size of the party warrants. The pots can be light aluminum, or suitable large-size cans, with bails either built in or improvised, and with a lid or two. It is preferable that the pots nest for carrying, but this is not essential. To prevent waste of space in the pack, they can be filled with small items and surrounded with clothing or food bags. The largest pot should hold at least a pint per person and the next largest should be nearly as large. If the pots are too tall and narrow, it will take a long time to heat the contents; if too shallow, the contents will spill. The ideal shape is the compromise that will also fit both the pack and the grate or plate. Be sure to bring a stirring spoon long enough to keep the soup thumb-free.

Expedients. Simplicity being the virtue that it is, we recommend that you pursue it in the wilderness kitchen. The simplest utensils are cans; a large juice can sits within a two-pound coffee can, which in turn nests in a No. 10 can. A "billycan grabber"—bought or improvised—allows you to use any can without a handle. A can may be set on the ground and a fire built around it, leaving no sooted stones to mark the spot and making way for the campfire later.

Food bags. Nearly all grub except butter should be stowed in waterproof food bags. The ideal fabric for making such bags is lightweight nylon coated with polyvinyl chloride (Koroseal). Any lightweight plastic-coated fabric is satisfactory provided the coating does not disintegrate when in contact with animal fat. A sample can be smeared with bacon grease and left for a few days as a test. Three sizes of bags plus one oversize bag to cover sooty pots are desirable. These bags can be made on the sewing machine at home. Length should be twice width, and tape (not draw string) should be sewed on to the edge seam $\frac{1}{2}$ inch below the open end.

As a final reminder: going light requires the saving of every unnecessary ounce and the elimination of every unnecessary article. It is easy to overload.

7. Map and Compass

WE DO NOT WANT the novice to feel that he must go back to school or take a correspondence course in map reading before he can safely have fun in the mountains. Many trips are open to the person who knows no more about cartography than how to interpret a road map roughly. Only a sketch map showing the current status of trails—their route and length—is required to plan a wilderness trail trip. One can sometimes consult a local expert on the chosen terrain, make a few notes of place names and distances, and get by with no map at all. There will probably be reasonably accurate trail signs to follow. Do not avoid wilderness travel because you do not have experience with map and compass. Ask a few questions and start out, taking due caution not to go over your head.

However, if you have no experienced leader and can find no local expert; if you would like to try some cross-country travel; if you would like to have the fun of planning your route on paper, of knowing where you are and what you are seeing and exactly where you are going next; and if you want the satisfaction of displaying a map on which the trails and routes you have covered are prominently marked—then you should become proficient in map reading.

A great deal has been written about the use of map and compass. Our emphasis is directed toward developing the ability to visualize the land from the map, and the map from the land. Nothing in map reading is more important. This was borne out time and again in World War II. It too often happened that military men crowded their minds with memorized signs and symbols and were not able to tell quickly, if at all, where they were on the map.

Study of the technicalities of map reading cannot sub stitute for practice in the field with map in hand. Therefore, we suggest the following steps in learning to know maps:

1) Obtain the United States Geological Survey's topographic map of the terrain in which you live, or of mountainous country with which you are familiar. These maps may be obtained from Superintendent of Documents, Washington, D.C., and are worth far more than the modest sum charged. An index map of the state or states in which you wish to travel should be requested to enable you to select the desired sheets.

2) Fold the map, face out, along the east-west center line. Accordion-fold vertically into four parts, with the northeast corner on top to keep the quadrangle name visible. The resulting size is convenient for home use and filing. For field use, accordion-fold the map again into four parts along east-west lines to an easy pocket size. This method of folding increases the convenience of using the map, particularly in the wind, because any part can be examined by merely opening folds, without re-folding. The exposed face of the map will get dirty, but a new map costs only a few cents—if you can bear to part with a map which has traveled enough to become colorful.

3) From the legend on the back of the map and from the marginal data on the bottom of the face learn the few symbols, the scale, and the contour interval which are needed in order to interpret the topography and culture properly.

4) Now become familiar with the contour topography on your map by repeated comparison with the terrain so that you no longer see it as a collection of lines, but as a relief map.

If you wish to become quickly familiar with extreme types of terrain, you may wish to add to your collection the finest topographic maps the Geological Survey has produced: Yosemite Valley Special Sheet (for cliff sculpture), Mount Rainier National Park (for glaciers), Grand Canyon (for desert land forms). You may even want to requisition one of the walls of your home, put these maps up on a temporary mounting and live with them for a while. They are good company and will afford welcome and rewarding diversion from the things you ought to be doing.

5) It is usually desirable to supplement the Geological Survey sheets with other maps which lack topography but are up to date on information about trails and other culture. You will note that the topographic maps are often obsolete in this respect. Forest Service and Park Service maps provide this information for most of the public domain in which you will wish to travel light.

6) Once one has mastered reasonably well the relation of contour lines to land forms, he can begin to interpolate the things that the map does not record. Observations of snow depth, forage, and forest cover in a limited area enable one to predict from the map which parts of the route are likely to be blocked by snow, where stock may feed, or where timberline may restrict high camps. For

example, if the map shows a place where a stream meanders, the ground must be nearly level there. In the mountains this means a meadow. Campsites and feed for pack animals would not be certain but would probably be found.

Unless three dimensional aerial photos (available for some mountain areas through the U.S. Forest Service) are used, even the best of the maps do not take away all the fun of pioneering. A pass may look easy when depicted with 100-foot contours yet may turn out to be blocked by a sheer 50-foot bluff. The topographer may have overlooked a lake, or may have drawn in freehand a slope that he could not see. A trail may have disappeared without a trace, a spring or stream may have gone dry, or a miner's cabin may long since have fallen under heavy snow. Such discrepancies may fascinate or irritate the map reader; in either event he knows he can always find his way back.

Orientation

In order to identify terrain features and follow one's progress on a map several simple skills must be learned. For effective field use, a map should usually be oriented so that the directions on map and terrain correspond. Several methods are possible:

1) It is easiest to orient a map from your known position and a known landmark and it is seldom necessary to use another method. Simply place a match vertically on the map over your position and another over the landmark; rotate the map and sight across the matches until they align with the landmark, and the map is oriented accurately.

2) If no landmarks can be identified, use a compass: Keeping the north-south line of the compass case parallel to a north-south line on the map, rotate the map and com-

pass until the needle coincides with the declination (see below) shown on the map. All map and ground directions will then coincide.

3) Lacking a compass, you may orient your map after determining south by use of a watch and the sun: Point the hour hand (at local standard time) toward the sun; south is about halfway between the hour hand and 12. For greater accuracy, use this method at mid-day.

To find your position, assuming that you don't know it but can recognize three landmarks: Place a match near the center of a sheet of thin paper; sight across to another match lined up with one landmark and draw a straight line in that direction; without moving the paper sight across the center match to each of the other landmarks and draw similar lines; place the paper over the map and move it until all three lines will, on the map, pass through the three landmarks. The center point is your position. Orient by rotating the map with any of the landmarks as in (1) above.

Two recognizable landmarks will serve if you have a compass (and the landmarks are separated by an approximate right angle). Orient the map by compass; place a match vertically on the map above one of the landmarks and move another match along the near edge of the map until it aligns with the actual landmark; draw a line between the two matches; repeat the process for the other landmark; the intersection of the two lines will be your approximate position. The use of a third landmark reduces your error.

To identify unknown landmarks reverse the procedure for identifying position. If there is only one line of sight, the position of the landmark is determinable only if you can judge its distance, recognize its shape from the map, and read its position with reference to intervening ridges.

Compass

In order to orient a map with a compass it is necessary to understand magnetic declination. The compass needle does not point to the north pole (true north) but to the magnetic north pole, which is north of Cincinnati and about 1,300 miles short of the north pole. Consequently, magnetic north is east of true north when one is in the West, and vice versa. The difference between true and magnetic north is called declination. To obtain a true map reading in the West, add the declination to the magnetic reading.

In a pinch, the bearing of the North Star may be taken as true north, and by day the sun may be used as explained above.

Compass bearing. To determine a bearing on a map, center the compass over the point on the map from which the bearing is to be taken, and orient the map. Then read the bearing where a line from the center of the compass to the actual object crosses the dial readings of the compass.

Compasses are marked according to two major systems. The azimuth system is easier to use and standard with the U.S. armed forces; in it the bearings are the degrees of a circle marked clockwise from north. A northwest bearing would be given as 315°.

Most civilian surveying is based upon four segments of the circle, graduated from north and south 90° in each direction to east and west; thus a northwest bearing would be given as north 45° west.

Plotting bearings. Center the compass over the point on the map from which the bearing was taken, orient the map, and project a line through the graduation on the compass which corresponds to the bearing. The point to which the bearing is taken will be on that line if the reading and plotting are accurate.

Traveling by compass. Traveling by compass is not often necessary, but can, on occasion, be very important. In restricted forest, in fog, or under other conditions of poor visibility, you must rely upon the accuracy of the compass, allowing for any local magnetic influence. Remember, however, that under stress your sense of direction may be off as much as 180° and unless you have previously marked on the compass case which end of the needle is north, the compass will seem to confirm your nonsense of direction.

Orient the map and determine the bearing on the first leg of your route. Then locate on that bearing a landmark as far as you can see and proceed toward it for the distance required. If the landmark is likely to be obscured for any reason, choose an intermediate spot on the same line before the distant one vanishes.

If no landmarks can be seen the last man should then direct the travel by compass, sighting on those ahead to a straight line. If you must turn to pass a cliff or ford a stream, return to the original line by recording the new angle of direction (a right angle is easiest) and the distance covered; a shorter but less accurate method is to leave the original course diagonally, clear the obstacle, and return at the same angle to your course and with the same number of paces, once the obstacle is passed.

Summer visibility is usually so good that the use of a compass is rarely required except, perhaps, to orient a map. Nevertheless, if there is any chance of getting lost in a prolonged storm or in dense forests, or in darkness when travel is necessary, one should have a compass and know how to use it. The best counsel is to take any old camp in a storm, or in heavy fog or darkness, and stay snug there.

8. Mountain Medicine

IT IS SURPRISING how infrequently accident and illness befall the hiker. Yet once in a while something does happen, and since you can't phone the family doctor, you have to know what to do. It is wise if at least one person on the trip has had first-aid training. The American Red Cross courses in this field are recommended. Their *First Aid Text-Book* might become a handy book to have along, and the weight is not prohibitive, especially if animals are carrying the packs. Specialized help will often be several days' travel away, and so you may be forced to practice some "second aid" in addition to first aid. Remember this general rule: the body tries to heal itself and will do so if it is protected and gently guided.

It is a general misconception that any who venture far from the end of the road must be rugged and tough. You don't have to be an Atlas to carry a pack nor a Hercules to climb the mountains. You should be in reasonably sound health and not too far out of condition. Try out your muscles a few times near home before taking off for the wilderness. It is especially important to break in new boots before the first day on the trail.

Blisters

It is easier to prevent blisters than to cure them. In breaking in boots some people find that wearing two pairs of socks helps reduce rubbing; an inner pair of silk hose is recommended. If an area begins to hurt, remove your boot and socks immediately and cover the tender spot with a patch of adhesive tape. Do it when you suspect that you are getting a blister, not when you think you have one.

In spite of all advice on the prevention of blisters, there is always someone who develops a fine crop. To treat a blister, sterilize a needle and the skin of the blister, and prick the blister at its edge, releasing the fluid. When the fluid is all drained out, leave the skin intact and cover the blister and surrounding skin with a patch of adhesive tape. Do not put gauze or cotton between the tape and the blister, unless the skin has already been pulled off, but plaster the tape directly on the blister. Leave it there and don't pull it off, or the loose skin will come off leaving a raw spot. At least five days is required for healing.

Sunburn

In the higher altitudes the ultraviolet rays are stronger and sunburn occurs more easily. Until a good coat of tan is obtained, protection should be provided, either by clothing or by medicaments. People with very tender skin sometimes find it necessary to block out all rays by using zinc oxide ointment or actors' makeup. Many sunburn lotions and creams have recently been put on the market; whether these are effective or not depends a great deal on individual needs, and they should be given previous trial.

Sunburn should be treated in the same way as any burn. The red area, provided it has not blistered, may be covered with any soothing ointment; for example, Antipyrexol or Mentholatum. If blisters occur, they should be treated with a bland ointment, such as boric acid ointment, and covered with a gauze dressing until healed. Treat the raw burn as an open cut. Put on a dressing to keep the dirt out, and it will heal itself.

Burns. What has been said on the treatment of sunburn applies as well to burns caused by any hot agent.

Snow blindness

The amount of snow encountered in the summertime is usually not sufficient to cause snow blindness. At very high elevations, however, it is possible to travel for several hours, even all day, on snow fields, and under such conditions—especially if the sun is bright—the eyes may be burned and snow blindness may result. This is a very painful and distressing affliction. Adequate dark glasses can prevent it. If no glasses are available, tie a bandanna over the eyes with a very small hole cut in front of each eye.

If snow blindness occurs, the eyes must be bandaged and rested until pain and spasm are relieved—probably for several days. Apply cold compresses over the closed lids for from 15 to 20 minutes at a time, putting drops of a bland oil such as castor or mineral oil in the eyes, or irrigating them with boric acid solution several times a day gives some relief. (See *Manual of Ski Mountaineering* for more detailed discussion.)

Lacerations

Cuts can vary in size and seriousness from small clean knife cuts to the large, deep, jagged cuts made by falling rocks. Treatment may vary from the application of a band-aid to a complicated repair.

First stop the flow of blood. Firm pressure of a compress over the wound is almost always enough to stop the flow; raising the injured part higher than the body will help. Don't use a tourniquet unless you have to, and even then only if you are skilled in its use. (It is my own belief that in *every* wound the blood flow can be stopped by pressure alone and that the tourniquet should be discarded.—H.S.K.)

When the laceration is larger than a band-aid can cover, special methods should be used. If medical aid is available within 12 hours, cover the wound with a compress and go to that aid. If it is not, wash the wound with a salt solution until all visible dirt particles are removed, if that is possible. Prepare the salt solution by dissolving 2 level teaspoonfuls of ordinary salt for each quart of boiling water, and use when cooled.

After irrigating the wound with salt solution, apply skin antiseptic (see below) to the skin only; press the edges of the cut together and fasten as adequately as possible with adhesive "butterflies" (see figure) ; apply sterile gauze dressing; and bandage firmly. If the wound is large or much contaminated with dirt, take penicillin tablets— V tablets, 250 milligrams each, four times a day. They are best taken with water on an empty stomach. *Some people become allergic to penicillin and may develop a serious reaction. Ask the victim about his previous experience and withhold penicillin if he has any knowledge of previous reaction.*

[NOTE: There is nothing static, it seems, about the so called wonder drugs. Research is always turning up some new facet—sometimes not too good—of last year's sure cure. Ask your own physician; keep current!—ED.]

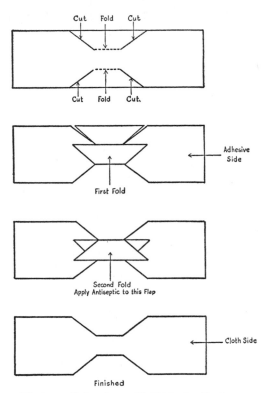

The butterfly bandage with 1½-inch adhesive tape.
From *Manual of Ski Mountaineering.*

Fractures and dislocations

Fractures of the extremities must be immobilized with splints. The Velpeau bandage is considered preferable for immobilization of the upper arm and shoulder, and padded

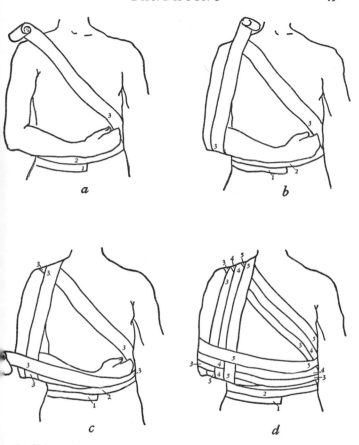

The Velpeau bandage (modified). Begin with two turns (1, 2) around waist, rolling toward affected side; bring third turn upward across chest, down behind shoulder and arm, upward over shoulder, across the back, and horizontally across forearm (3). More turns can be applied (4, 5), depending on desired stability of arm and length of bandage roll. From *Manual of Ski Mountaineering.*

splints for the forearm. It is best to use traction splints on fractures of the thigh and lower leg, but such splints are rarely available in the wilderness, and padded splints must be improvised. Sides of boxes or kyacks can be utilized for the shorter splints. It is more difficult to improvise suitable splints for thigh fractures, where longer splints are necessary, since long saplings are often too supple and larger trees too heavy and bulky. Perhaps the easiest course is to make camp for the injured person where he lies and send for a suitable splint. This, of course, may not be possible on a mountain ridge, and each case must be considered individually and that procedure followed which will cause least damage.

For the technique of splint application, see the *American Red Cross First Aid Text-Book*.

In a compound fracture additional care must be taken. If possible, the skin surrounding the wound should be washed with soap and water and the wound and bone irrigated with two quarts of clean salt water (the preparation of which is described under Lacerations). The skin around the wound—but not the open wound and bone—should be painted with a skin antiseptic (for example, 2 per cent tincture of iodine or a commercially prepared mercurial antiseptic). If the limb is greatly out of alignment, gentle traction is exerted and the limb made straight. Sometimes protruding ends of bone will be pulled inside the flesh. This, of course, protects them, but at the same time will bury dirt if it is not already removed. Be diligent in your preparation to prevent this. The wound should then be covered with sterile gauze, bandaged, and the limb splinted. The injured person should take penicillin tablets by mouth immediately. (See page 77.)

Injuries to joints

Often it is not possible to distinguish a sprain from a fractured joint, unless X-ray examination is made. Only when the injury appears to be so slight that the additional support of tape would allow the victim to travel without undue discomfort may the joint be taped and further use allowed. For all joint injuries, a doctor should be consulted as soon as possible in order to avert any permanent disability which might otherwise result.

Dislocations should be considered fractures until proved otherwise and splinted as simple fractures are.

If the shoulder of a victim who knows the injury is recurrent is dislocated, an exception to this rule may be made, and the dislocation reduced in the following way: place the injured person on his side in a horizontal position, his injured shoulder down so that the arm can hang down freely below him. Tie a weight of about ten pounds to the wrist. In from 30 to 45 minutes the shoulder muscles should tire enough to permit the dislocation to reduce itself. If they do not, treat the injury as a simple fracture and seek medical aid as soon as possible. A Velpeau bandage is recommended for the immobilization of a dislocated shoulder.

Shock

With any of the severe injuries described above, shock is a common accompaniment. Prevention of shock is easier than its cure. To prevent shock, the injured person should be laid down, head lower than feet, and should be kept comfortably warm. Do not overheat the victim in your zeal to prevent shock. A good rule is to make him comfortable. If extra clothing is necessary, use it. If he is too hot, some of his clothing may be removed. Prevent the

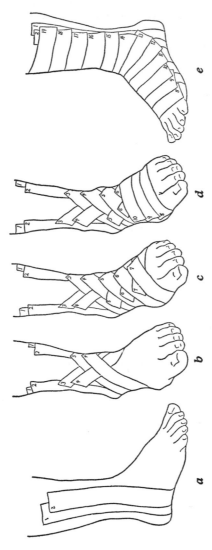

Taping an ankle (see text). (a) Two adhesive stirrups are applied, extending one-third the way up each side of the lower leg. (b) Stirrup-like strips are continued forward down the foot, crossing over ankle and instep. (c) Strips are continued down to the base of the toes on the sole. (d) Layer of strips is applied over the top of the foot, starting at the base of the toes, crossing from side to side. (e) The strips are continued up the foot, ankle, and leg to the top of the first two stirrups. From *Manual of Ski Mountaineering.*

victim from perspiring since salt is thus lost from the blood, and the blood is brought to the skin, being deflected from the general circulation and from important organs, where it is badly needed.

As every first-aider knows, the injured person should be moved as little as possible and then only with caution, so that he will not be injured further.

To minimize shock, pain must be relieved. Capsules of codeine sulfate (1 grain) and aspirin (5 grains) obtained on prescription will help relieve pain and should be included in the medical supplies. Aspirin may cause perspiration and should be used with caution, not more than once every four to six hours. If morphine is available, a $\frac{1}{4}$-grain tablet may be dissolved under the tongue every four hours for severe pain.

Hot tea, coffee, or chocolate is helpful when the patient is able to take and retain it, but avoid giving too much fluid, since it will then become necessary for the patient to empty his bladder—extremely difficult if he is supine.

Heat stroke and exhaustion

Exposure to high temperatures may have such diverse effects as heat cramps, exhaustion, or stroke.

Heat cramps occur in people who perspire profusely, thereby losing salt and water from the blood. The cramps are characterized by spasms of the muscles of the arms and legs and abdomen, and may be prevented or cured by drinking salt water (1 teaspoonful of salt per gallon of water) or by taking salt tablets.

In heat exhaustion, weakness, dizziness, profuse perspiration, and weak and rapid pulse occur, in addition to the cramps. There is rarely loss of consciousness. Treatment consists of rest in a cool place, the maintenance of body warmth, and the intake of saline or sweet drinks.

In heat stroke or sunstroke the heat-regulating mechanism of the body is overwhelmed. The onset is often rapid and consciousness is lost early. The face is flushed, the skin hot and dry. The temperature is elevated, often to a severe degree. The pulse is strong and rapid. Treatment is heroic and consists of cold-water baths or sprays and even ice enemas. As the temperature is reduced, cold sponge baths should be given.

Snake bites

Many people are hysterically afraid of snakes. Beneficial snakes are frequently mistaken for poisonous ones and killed. Often hikers are petrified with fear on going into "snake country." This fear is greatly exaggerated. Snakes will retreat when approached by humans and will bite only as a last resort. Most bites occur when the snake is unable to flee, and, like any cornered animal, strikes to defend.

In the Far West the most dangerous poisonous snake is the rattler, of which there are several species. The Sonoran coral snake is found in the southern desert regions of Arizona and New Mexico, but it is nocturnal, is seldom seen, and rarely bites man. The rattler is found in California from low deserts up to elevations of 7,000 feet; occasionally one may be found as high as 10,000 feet. Rattlers prefer the shade under brush and rocks, although they may bask in the sun on the tops of rocks for short periods of time. They don't mind streams.

The venom of these snakes is poisonous to humans, but the seriousness of a snake bite depends on the size of the person bitten and on the amount of venom injected. This latter is determined by the size and age of the snake, whether it has recently fed and thus recently expended its reserve of venom, and on the degree of penetration of the fangs. When all these variables are taken into account, it is evident that a lethal dose of venom is rare.

The venom of the rattlesnake causes severe local pain, progressive swelling, hemorrhage, gangrene, and local infection of the wound. After severe bites, general reactions are hemorrhage in the internal organs, shock, vomiting, and collapse of the circulatory system.

The venom of the coral snake acts primarily on the nervous system. There is little local pain and no swelling. There may be local numbness. In a few hours after severe bites there is paralysis of speech, swallowing, eye movement, and breathing.

Treatment. Following a bite by a poisonous snake, physical activity should be avoided if possible, since this accelerates the absorption and dissemination of the venom. If the bite is on an extremity, a constricting band should be applied immediately about one inch above the bite. It should only be tight *enough to stop the venous circulation,* AND THAT IS NOT VERY TIGHT, not nearly so tight as is the practice in the application of the tourniquet to check arterial bleeding. It should be loosened every 15 to 20 minutes to avoid complete venous stagnation.

The fang punctures are then incised by a sharp blade after the application of a skin antiseptic over and around the bite. Short criss-cross or closely parallel incisions are made about ¼ inch long and definitely through the skin. Light suction is then applied to the wounds. This is most easily done with small specially designed suction cups. If mouth suction is necessary, the mouth should be rinsed frequently; for although swallowed venom is neutralized by stomach juices, some absorption through cuts in the mouth can occur. Suction from each incision should be maintained for from 30 to 40 minutes out of each hour, and continued in this manner for about 15 hours.

As the swelling extends, the tourniquet should be replaced just beyond the advancing margin. Incisions are made in a circular pattern about the bite and as the swelling spreads, additional cuts are made around the limb so that suction may be applied to the new areas of involvement. The amount of bloody fluid obtained from the incisions is small at first, but contains more concentrated venom than do the larger amounts that appear later. Hot, wet, common-salt or Epsom-salt compresses are applied to the entire extremity when it is not necessary to have the area exposed. When available, use antivenin for rattlesnake bites. None is made for coral-snake venom.

Snake venom lowers resistance to infection; penicillin should be taken (see p. 77) as soon as possible.

General treatment for shock is important. The traditional use of large doses of whiskey is dangerous and can definitely be condemned. The use of potassium permanganate or other chemicals has not been successful.

Mountain sickness.

Many individuals who spend most of the year near sea level will develop mountain sickness if they ascend rapidly to high elevations without first acclimatizing themselves. Apparently fatigue may bring on an attack in a person who, if he had remained quiet, would have suffered no ill effects. The symptoms are headache, nausea—often with vomiting—dizziness, feeling of illness, and weakness. Sometimes the bowels are upset and a persistent diarrhea occurs. The onset of symptoms may occur many days after arrival at high altitudes, depending upon the degree of exertion and fatigue. No particular treatment is necessary except rest. Acclimatization occurs within a few days; if it does not and symptoms persist, it is best that the person return to lower altitudes and remain there.

It should be mentioned here that many of the normal body functions, especially in women, are upset temporarily by changes in altitude, and such disturbances should not cause great concern.

Swimming

Swimmers can meet with as many accidents in the streams and lakes of the mountains as they can in pools and rivers at lower elevations, and should swim in compliance with the safety rules practiced elsewhere. In addition, it must be remembered that one's wind is much shorter at high altitudes, the water is colder, cramps are more frequent, and exhaustion comes sooner. With this in mind, don't swim out toward the center of a lake, but swim along the shore.

Water sterilization

Fortunately the sources of streams in our wilderness areas are usually uncontaminated, and one need not sterilize the drinking and cooking water. However, if one is traveling in a semipopulated area or in a foreign country, it is safer to take the precaution of using Halazone tablets in the drinking water and of boiling the cooking water. One Halazone tablet is dissolved in one quart of water and allowed to stand thirty minutes. The iodine tablet "Bursoline" is considered superior to Halazone; one in one quart of water renders it potable in fifteen minutes.

Immunization

All persons should have active immunization against tetanus—especially those handling stock. A yearly tetanus booster just before a trip is recommended; this obviates necessity for a booster after an injury on the trip.

9. Women

HITTING THE TRAIL is by no means a game for men only. The doe is quite as well adapted to her environment as the stag. Women and girls can cope with weather, bugs, bears, and topography with perfect confidence and success even when they go on hen parties without the aid of any male horse-sense or muscle at all. What it takes is know-how, and precisely the same advice that applies to men and boys should be assimilated by women and girls. However, the information offered in the other chapters of this manual can be modified and supplemented by a few strictly feminine items.

To begin with, test your capacity for hard exercise and exposure on easy trips before undertaking anything too strenuous. Do not go along with a bunch of cannonballs whose ambitions run to great distances, great altitudes, and burning speed, or who are setting out to conquer some major objective, unless you know your ability to keep up. You might thereafter be classified as a ball-and-chain. However, when recreation and inspiration are the objectives, many trips can be adapted to individual capacities by so arranging the itinerary that those more strenuously inclined can make side trips or go cross-country while others stay on the trail. The social advantages of a good mixed company may outweigh the importance of an ambitious itinerary.

It is very desirable to go through a schedule of physical training before an anticipated trip, particularly if you are going to a high altitude. This does not mean merely one or two short hikes. It means several hikes of increasing length carrying a pack and wearing the same shoes that you will wear on your trip so that they will be thoroughly tested and broken in. In addition, a regular schedule of frequent vigorous short walks or other outdoor exercise is highly recommended.

Your potential ability to stand such vicissitudes as heat and cold and short rations is as good as the average man's, and as a rock-hopper, log-balancer, and rough-trail-scrambler, you can also compete quite favorably with Mr. Average-Man. There is one respect, however, in which you must allow yourself to be inferior: you can't carry so heavy a pack. So you have *got* to learn to "keep it light." This is highly desirable whether you have to carry it yourself, or whether you can induce some burro or husband to carry it for you, since in the one case, your back will suffer and in the other, your reputation. The number of pounds that a woman can carry depends so much upon her size, muscular strength, and physical condition that limits cannot be prescribed. The practicable load limit for different individuals seems to vary more for women than for men. However, 25 pounds seems to be the absolute upper load limit for all but the extraordinarily husky woman. The person who considers herself of average "outdoor-girl type" strength may carry 35 pounds on 4-to-5-day trips, but the extra 10 pounds will almost certainly diminish the buoyancy and joyousness of her gait by several hundred per cent, and, once home, she will not undertake such a trip again except under extreme duress.

A poorly fitted pack will greatly decrease the feasible load limit, and women are likely to handicap themselves by borrowing men's or boys' packs when they do not possess properly fitted packs of their own. Female backs and shoulders differ from the male in contour and proportions as well as in size. It is very desirable to acquire a pack of one's very own, of a size to accommodate one's own normal weight-load, and if necessary to have it altered or shaped to suit one's own peculiarities.

It might be better to substitute for the female of the species, in place of a clothing and equipment list, a list of what not to take. However, this would take several volumes and would exceed the scope of this manual. So turn to the list of clothing and personal effects in the chapter on equipment and if you are tempted to add anything to that list, consider carefully at least three times whether you really need it. Most women will be sorely tempted to take more changes of clothing than they really need. In the first place, washing and drying clothes is normally very easy in camp. You simply wash them out quickly when you bathe each evening provided you don't make camp too late, and they dry very fast in the mountains. In the second place, women must learn to consider the difference between the three distinct sets of values which underlie the modern urge to cleanliness, one being comfort, the second hygiene, and the third being the spit-'n-polish aesthetic standard. The second and third requirements vanish when you hit the trail. The dirt you will encounter in the wilderness is perfectly sanitary, being rendered so by oxygen and remoteness from human habitation. The spit-'n-polish aesthetic standard becomes so impracticable as to appear even slightly ridiculous. Aesthetic values will lie more in your surroundings than in your person. There remains only the valid objective of comfort. Clothes that have been sweat-soaked become clammy.

Women seem, in general, to be more susceptible to cold feet than men, so have clean socks (dust is O.K., but not perspiration) to wear on cold nights.

The clothing list in the chapter on equipment covers most of what you need to know, but a few special comments are in order. Blue jeans are widely accepted in the West as the most practical, sturdy, cheap pant. Regular boys' jeans are likely to be tight in the crotch and big in the waist if you are normally endowed. Different models vary in cut and some may fit you. If not, there are special jeans made just like men's, but cut for women. Women's ready-made slacks are too flimsy, but there are frontier pants available in heavy denim that are good.

Many women are prone to chafe on the inside of the thigh on long hikes. This can be prevented by undershorts of soft material, and with legs that come part way down the thigh, in place of briefs.

The biggest problem is likely to be shoes. Most hiking boots made for women seem still to be modeled on the lasts that were manufactured when women hiked in long skirts or voluminous bloomers. They have knee-height tops, pointed toes, and too much heel. If you are fortunate enough to have a wide foot, particularly if your heel is wide, you will be able to buy boys' shoes that will be satisfactory. If you have a narrow foot, your problem may be difficult indeed. Leather-top basketball shoes make good hiking shoes if you can find them. Canvas-top shoes (above the ankles) are much better than poorly fitted leather shoes. If you have to buy high-top boots, have the tops cut off above the ankle or part way up the calf. Very high tops are hot, heavy, and unnecessary.

It is controversial whether women have more delicate skin than men, but even if you aren't the rose-petal type, bear in mind that strong sun and wind at high altitudes can wreak more havoc than you may think. Be sure to have adequate protection along for face, neck, and hands, in the form of brimmed hat, bandanna, gloves, cold cream or lanolin.

It goes without saying that you will not wish to tote a very elaborate assortment of cosmetics. If your skin is not naturally very oily, a lanolin preparation will provide the most efficient lubrication for it. Some women find this essential in addition to a sunburn preparation, for the preservation of a layer or two of face. Face powder is likely not to match after you have acquired either sunburn or tan, and besides, it cakes with perspiration. Even though you may shudder now at the thought of wearing a nude face, you will probably find after you have been out a couple of days that you like yourself best in just lipstick.

Under the heading of "strictly feminine and personal" comes some advice regarding your menstrual period. Whatever your individual peculiarities may be ordinarily, they may be quite different on a mountain hiking trip. You may be thrown off schedule and you may need lots more or lots fewer sanitary napkins than usual. Tampons worn internally may be more comfortable for hiking and will prevent the chafing that may be your lot with externally worn napkins (but for your first trip by all means have a supply of the kind you are used to). And don't forget, there are no rest rooms with vending machines where you are going.

Finally, one little luxury item. If you are curvaceous, dig a hole for your hips at night.

10. Especially for Men

[What follows was not written for a manual, and we think much would be lost if it were rewritten for a manual—in the how-to-do-it, 1-2-3-4 style a manual has to have if the reader is to be given a fair chance to find the points and paragraphs he is looking for. Nevertheless, Elizabeth S. Cowles, one of the country's foremost women mountaineers, long wanted to write about a subject that she felt almost evangelical about, a subject which has important bearing upon wilderness travel, as we think you will agree. What she finally wrote first appeared in the *Sierra Club Bulletin* for June 1949. We are happy to add it to these pages just as she wrote it, without the cloak of the semianonymous "we" that has necessarily been resorted to elsewhere in this book. As we say in our title for what she herself entitled "Have You a Mountain Widow in Your Home?" this is especially for men; we should prefer that women turn immediately to page 100 and thus avoid getting any ideas which could make them any more difficult to handle than they are.—Ed.]

I REALLY HATE to set myself up as a critic of the opposite sex. Men have always been among my best friends, especially the mountain-climbing variety. But there is one mistake they make so frequently that I feel impelled to point it out.

I'll begin with a story. It isn't a true story in that I never knew a mountaineer named Don, let alone one who

was married to a girl named Alice. But it may illustrate
the point I want to make as well as some of the true
stories I do know. I had met Don in the Tetons, we'll say.
He attached himself to our climbing brotherhood and
we had some fine times in the hills. He did his part on
the mountain and his part in camp and added to everybody's good time with an inexhaustible fund of vitality
and good humor. None of us thought of him as having a
wife. She wasn't around. She was back in Little Rock, it
turned out, waiting patiently for Don to come home.

Don't jump to the conclusion that Don and Alice were
unhappily married because they weren't. She was a perfect
dear and they were devoted to each other. Nor was Alice,
as you might think, the fragile type, not rugged enough
for the great outdoors. On the contrary, she had always
been something of an athlete. In fact, as Don confided to
me later, it was seeing her outplay and outlast an op-
ponent in a tennis tournament five years before that had
first bowled him over. The truth was, though I was some
time in finding it out, that Alice was just the kind of person for the mountains, as Don obviously was, but somehow they'd never succeeded in getting together about it.
Why?

It's a long story but I think I'll tell it. It all went back
to the honeymoon. Don had thought it would be fine to
take Alice climbing. There was a certain amount of un-
derstandable masculine vanity about it. He had watched
her shine on the tennis court—it was going to be nice to
have her see him do his stuff on a rock wall. And that she
would take to climbing like a duck to water he hadn't the
faintest doubt. I think Don fully expected Alice to swarm
up her first chimney like a human fly!

Sad to relate, things didn't turn out quite that way.

It was a funny thing: with anyone else but his new wife

Don would probably have known better than to go at their
first undertaking as if en route to a fire. But this time he
got carried away. Since he had a well-developed set of
climbing muscles himself, it apparently never crossed his
mind that training is something a sea-level spouse acquires
slowly. Nor did it occur to him, carrying eighty pounds
himself, that a twenty-five pound pack might be a bit
heavy for a beginner. And what a shame it was about
her blisters! Those new boots should have had an easier
breaking in. (So should Alice.) Bad luck hounded them,
too, in that five days of solid rain followed their installation in camp and she caught a fearful cold. It was a hide-
ous combination of the preventable and the unpreventable,
like most human disasters. But that wasn't all.

Don made his next mistake when finally the sun came
out. He rushed Alice off to a favorite cliff of his. Lost in
his own delight at being back among the familiar cracks
and ledges, he failed entirely to notice that Alice, to whom
such maneuvers were new, was having the living daylight
scared out of her. Mind you, she behaved very well. She
was a good sport about everything and tried her darnedest.
But the will-to-do, unfortunately, is not always enough.
The harder she tried the worse things got and finally her
weariness and fright were only exceeded by the appalling
depths of her sense of failure. It was quite a while before
Don, his head in the clouds, noticed how slow and unac-
countably awkward she was and that she didn't seem to
be enjoying herself at all. He was surprised at first, then
tenderly amused. But when matters failed to improve, his
feeling changed to one of very real disappointment and
chagrin. Poor Don, he had pictured it all so differently!
It never occurred to him, then or later, that there was only
one person responsible. That was himself.

Things went from bad to worse until—a break for Alice

—two Dartmouth classmates turned up in their valley. Don had one super-duper climb with them while Alice stayed in camp. Vacations were short in those war years. Soon our young couple were on their way back to civilization where they took up the threads of a life that proved to be very full and happy. But—and this is the point of the story—*Alice never went climbing again.* And who can blame her?

This fable illustrates an imaginary set of conditions and those, I grant you, may be rather exaggerated. But the general outline of the situation is so often seen as to be relatively common in mountaineering circles. The climbing widow abounds. She usually has to choose between waiting around on a hotel porch day after day while himself is off exercising in the hills or, worse still, being left out of his vacation plans entirely. All this is a great pity. As everyone knows or should know, the climber is at his very best in the mountains. He is happiest, healthiest, gayest, funniest. What a loss for people to miss this in the one they love! Companionship is a rich part of the climbing experience. Why impoverish married life by failing to share it?

I claim that it needn't be so. If your spouse has the necessary number of hands and feet, general good health and plenty of affection for you, it's just a matter of patience, imagination and a little salesmanship. I don't mean to say that the little woman will necessarily be able to wave an American flag beside you on the summit of K2, but the probabilities are she'll grow to love the mountains and share your joy in wild country if you'll only give her half a chance. And for the rest of your lives you'll have wonderful times in the hills together, to say nothing of the endless fun that will be yours of planning and recalling vacations future and past.

No wands, potions or abracadabra are necessary. It's all quite easy. You just have to obey a few simple rules when first you introduce your lady to the mountaineering scene.

Rule one is: *Don't let her get tired.*

Take it easy! Gear the proceedings to her strength. Resist the temptation to whip up a steep trail at a three mile an hour clip to start with. Make it a short walk, a gentle grade. Have a fine *Aussichtspunkt* (Deutsch for a place from which you get a lovely view) an hour or so out. Eat lunch there (and be sure to tell her how purty she looks against the sky in that red flannel shirt!). Keep your love happy and comfortable while she's gradually working up some hill-going muscles—and don't forget that it will take time. Details mustn't escape you, like seeing that boots fit so as to spare her the painful ordeal of blisters. Be sure she doesn't get a charley-horse, or pick up a terrible sunburn, or suffer unnecessary harassment from black flies or mosquitoes. Just remember (in time) that there are salt pills, lanolin preparations and insect dope available at the nearest drugstore.

When you are established in camp (and you might start her off, by the way, with a pack that is bulky—for her pride—but light) do a few extras so she'll be pleasantly surprised at how nice camping is, right from the beginning. If your dear one is to be cook, why not have given her a little chance to practice camp cookery ahead of time so that her first meal is good and she commences her new career with a sense of success?

That sense of success is, actually, the whole business, the secret of everything. Never forget it for a minute! She must always feel she's doing well, that you are pleased with her and delighted at her progress. If she truly feels this, she *will* do well, she *will* make progress (and you *will* be delighted—no make-believe about it!).

The importance of this sense-of-success cannot be over-emphasized. It is the *sine qua non*. Remember it especially in the second commandment: *Don't let her get scared*.

Take the real climbing very slowly. Build up her confidence with the greatest care. Try beginning with slab walking, the way the mountain troops do. It does wonders for the sense of balance and your lady-love will be far less inclined to grab and cling later, when the angle increases. On the first steep pitches, the going should be really easy with lots to hold on to. Vary the terrain, of course, and try her out on different types of assignments to keep it interesting. But never dream of undertaking anything at all difficult until she's entirely at home with simple chimneys, slabs and ledges and you're dead certain she's enjoying herself. That's the vital thing to watch out for: is she having a good time? If it continues to be fun for her, then you're a first-rate teacher and your pupil is bound to graduate eventually with honors.

That the advanced lessons in climbing have to be handled very carefully too goes without saying. You mustn't relax for a moment! Beginners shouldn't be asked to accustom themselves to exposure on a rock face, for instance, at the same time that they are learning to make a little go a long way in the line of holds. One lesson at a time, my friend. This goes too for the techniques of snow and ice work, for training in the use of rope and ice ax, and for the many other skills that advanced alpinism requires. If big-league mountaineering is what you enjoy, you'll want your wife to enjoy it too. It's all perfectly possible. But just remember how long it took you to learn the business and don't expect her to be a lot brighter than any one else in the world. Time, practice, patience and affection—combine these and it will surprise you how soon your lady begins to feel the exhilaration of the airiest maneuvers.

I might throw in a few extra tips here: *You* be the one that seems to be holding *her* back, not vice versa. It will be fine for the general morale. Praise her endlessly. It's wonderful what a compliment does to hearten us girls. And by all you hold dear, do NOT condescend! All will be lost if you sound like Paderewski instructing a first-year student of limited talent.

Now let's go on to commandment three: It is: *Don't let her get bored.*

Set yourself to making camping and climbing a delightful experience. It's poor judgment to stick out a seven-day rain, for instance—how much brighter it would be to take your girl-friend back to the valley where she could get a hot bath and go to the movies for a change. Vary your schedule: don't always be exercising wildly. Have frequent days off. Bring some good books along (the little paper-covered ones don't weigh very much) and read aloud. Introduce her to mountain photography, or learn about alpine flowers together, or see what the two of you can find out from one of the tiny bird handbooks and a pair of field glasses. A one-track mind in the hills is a fearful mistake. The mountain experience is rich—investigate some of the many and varied fields of interest it offers. You never know what may capture her fancy—and yours.

All this is likely to take some self-discipline to start with and you probably won't achieve many fancy ascents that first year—but I'll be willing to bet a substantial amount that you'll end by considering it one of the best investments you ever made. You'll reap rich rewards; so will she!

So far my remarks have been directed toward the mountaineering man who for some reason has failed to condition his wife in favor of his beloved sport. But now I'd like to put in a brief word to the climbing widow—

the one who stays home while her husband is off galli-
vanting in the Canadian Rockies and who perhaps feels a
little sorry for herself at times. Madam, it is not too late
—that is, if you *want* to do something about it.

The following story is short, it also happens to be true.
It concerns my own sister. In the early years of their
married life, her husband used to roar up steep trails a
mile a minute en route to the high peaks. Emmy followed,
usually in tears. Obviously Emmy wasn't destined to be
God's Gift to Alpinism, and so Mac took to going off on
climbing vacations by himself or with a like-minded pal.
But that was a long time ago. Things are different these
days. He still goes back to the hills whenever a busy law
practice permits but now Emmy goes along. Her alpine
aptitudes haven't changed any. She has, however, become
a strong trail and rough-country walker and loves it.
What's more, she's the best camp cook north of the Mason-
Dixon line. Lucky the climbers that start upward fortified
by Emmy's marvelous menus! Emmy cut her coat to suit
her cloth. She looked the facts in the eye and then worked
out her own personal answer. She knew what she wanted,
and what she wanted was to go along. So: she made herself essential in the pattern. You couldn't make Mac go to
the mountains without her. And she has a wonderful time.

One more thing occurs to me before closing. If you are
a high-altitude parent who would like your youngsters to
enjoy climbing: what I've written applies to children just
as much as it does to wives. See that they have a good
time in the hills, and take pains to adjust the schedule
and tempo to their strength and abilities. Give them from
the very beginning a sense of success and approval and
you'll find you have a bunch of climbing maniacs in your
family. They'll be at you all the time to take them into
the mountains. What a Utopia that would be!

11. Children

WHAT ABOUT you trail enthusiasts who have acquired small fry? Do you think you are condemned to remain within toddling distance of a summer cabin or automobile? Experience has proved that this is not necessary. Short hiking trips, burro trips of moderate propor tions, or excursions from a high country base camp are quite practicable provided itineraries are scaled down and other arrangements geared to meet the needs of the family. We say family rather than children because if your trip is too ambitious, it may be the parents who feel the strain first. The endurance or at least the resilience of healthy children may amaze you, and moreover, they enjoy advantages such as the absence of any aversion toward dirt or nudity which minimize nervous strain. The parents on the other hand have the responsibility of caring for the children minus the conveniences of home. Therefore, we advise you not to undertake the kind of itinerary that even the less zealous adult party would follow. Think as little as possible of long-range objectives beyond the availability of good campsites and feed for the animals, and try instead to recapture childish joy in aimless wandering and delight in all the wonders of the trail, great and small, from the loveliest, longest vista down to the queerest bug or the smallest flower. Go far enough into the wilderness to be free of intrusion by the civilized rabble and wander about sufficiently to enjoy fine changes of scenery and campsites. Beyond that, take it easy.

Child psychologists in recent years have been advancing ideas which may startle some city dwellers, though they seem only reasonable to wilderness lovers. For example, they suggest that it is very important for children to have the opportunity to live through some of the more primitive experiences of their earlier ancestors in contact with the elements and natural forces if their personalities are to develop fully and wholesomely. It is not our province to delve into psychological theory, but surely it is no more than the right of a child to be afforded some escape from the sheltered and mechanized existence imposed upon him by modern urban life, with its unnatural emphasis upon respect for man-made material property. So, consider the possibility that in taking your children on wilderness trips you may be affording them very positive benefits as well as affording yourselves the opportunity to enjoy your accustomed recreation.

The concern expressed above about the strain upon the parents should not overshadow all concern on behalf of the children. We do not believe that preschool-age children are likely to overdo seriously so long as they are given normal opportunity for rest and refreshment. However, their spirits will be kept up and irritability down and everyone's morale the better if rest and refreshment periods are adapted to their needs and inclinations rather than to a prearranged itinerary or to other considerations such as the fishing or the view. It should be borne in mind that children pour out great stores of energy in play and run-about activity as well as on the trail and they rest when they are tired and not because there is a long climb ahead. Older children, on the other hand, who have developed ambitions to perform feats of endurance such as the scaling of high mountains in conscious competition with their elders, are sometimes capable of really harmful overexertion and some restraint may have to be put upon them. This will depend upon the child's physical health and preconditioning, upon his rivalry among members of the group in the performance of mountaineering feats or in the prestige attached to such performances which might prod the youngster into efforts too heroic for his years. Of course, these admonitions apply particularly at high altitudes.

A good plan if children are small is to move camp only in the mornings and eat lunch at the new campsite. Then settle down for a leisurely afternoon, and children can take naps if they will.

A small child riding on his father's back (see below) as a rule cannot ride happily for more than 2 hours without a break.

The optimum age for introducing a child to the rigors of camping will depend upon the eagerness of the parents and perhaps upon the temperament of the child. We know of an infant of 6 months and a child of 18 months who became campers apparently with satisfaction to all concerned. We also know of another who began at 17 months, but quite frankly we would not wish to repeat that *tour de force*. He is a restless, very active youngster, and the energies of 4 adults were largely absorbed in keeping track of him. Every time he was put upon the ground he toddled headlong away from camp, it seemed in all directions at once, and rarely returned without being dragged or carried. He climbed logs and boulders from which he might have fallen and broken his skull, vanished from sight in foxholes and became entangled in thickets. Torrential rivers and precipitous cliffs held a lethal attraction for him. Therefore, we would prefer to initiate a child after he became subject to some degree of verbal guidance and could be called back to camp or away from danger.

Avoid rattlesnake country if possible and take maximum precautions against snake bite. The consequences of snake bite can be much more serious to a child than to an adult. A dose of poison goes farther in a small body than in a large one, and children are more likely to be bitten about the body or face which is far more serious and difficult to treat than bites on a limb.

Most children nowadays who are under routine medical care are inoculated for tetanus. They should be inoculated or given a booster before your trip.

There are other risks involved in leaving civilization, such as the absence of medical care in case of sickness. However, there are compensations such as the absence of civilized contamination—often the cause of sickness.

The grub list may be modified somewhat, though most items on typical camp grub lists are suitable for children beyond the infant diet stage. We have known children to drink milk made of milk powder in enormous quantities and without the slightest objection. Others have refused it during an entire trip, but have perhaps made up for it by eating large quantities of whole-milk cheese which provided essentially the same nutrients. Canned custards and packaged puddings can help make up the milk requirements. A child who dislikes powdered milk may find hot chocolate or "chocolate milk shake," quickly made with instant cocoa powder, acceptable. For a very small child, the canned puréed baby foods are convenient to use and have the advantage of being a familiar form of food to the child, so we believe they should be taken even though the regular grub lists advise against much canned food on account of its weight. Frequent snacks are fine "pick-me-ups" for children who are leading a more than usually strenuous life. Many children exhibit less fatigue and better spirits if substantial food, including such solid items as meat and cheese, is always available to them upon the slightest whim of appetite, though never urged upon them.

Special equipment will depend upon the age and individual. But we can make some general comments.

Some children, like some adults, will require more protection against sun, heat, and cold than others. In general, remember that their skins are young and relatively tender and that they have less sense about protecting themselves than do adults (though there are adults who are exceptions to this statement). So, if in doubt about your child's requirements, err on the side of too much protection in the form of warm clothing, hats with wide brims, sunburn preventive, etc. Some agent such as calamine lotion to treat and prevent chafing may be helpful.

We know of no commercial source of children's sleeping bags. A child's-size bag is desirable to save weight, but is not necessary as children can use ordinary sleeping bags, preferably the narrow mummy-case type. A child's bag can be homemade from inexpensive lightweight sheet blankets, folded and filled with wool bat. Stitch or tie the wool at intervals to insure even distribution. Then cut a modified mummy case to size, not too snug as most children resent being closely confined, cut an opening in front for the head and insert a zipper. Such a bag is washable.

Plenty of mosquito netting to cover the children both waking and sleeping is important and is better than mosquito dope (too easily rubbed into the eyes).

A harness with leash in which to strap and hold a small child may give great aid and comfort to a mother when a trail traverses the brink of a precipice or the bank of a roaring river.

In addition to standard equipment, it will be wise with preschool-age children to take along some portions of the home environment whose value is purely emotional, even at the expense of inconvenience and irreparable damage to the articles; these might be, for example, teddy bears, toys, books, familiar clothes, or eating utensils. We know of one child who, at the age of a year and a half, took among other things his favorite blanket, which happened to be an angelic shade of pink, and as soft and fluffy as a cloud. That was before the trip. During the trip, it was used day and night, as a cocoon, as a tarpaulin, a towel, a rug, a toga, a ball, and a rag. It became grimy, faded, dirty, gray, and as compact and hard as canvas, but the emotional comfort it provided during an otherwise total change in material environment was well worth the sacrifice of a very beautiful blanket. Incidentally it was apparently just as comforting even in the latest stages of its metamorphosis as it was in the beginning.

There are two modes of transportation for children too young to walk far, namely, father and burro. The younger ones can be carried on their fathers' backs beginning at the age of about 18 months and until they are too heavy to carry or until they are old enough to be trusted on donkey back. One baby of 6 months was transported in a basket fastened as a kyack to a burro's pack saddle.

A saddle for riding a father can be made by cutting leg-holes in the corners of a small rucksack (with frame). The stitches in the seams can be cut without cutting the material. Or a child's car seat, preferably with tray, can be mounted on a rucksack frame. Either of these rigs pro-

vides a head rest so that the child can sleep with father
providing the cradle motion. Clever fathers may invent
other devices.

An older child can ride on top of a donkey packed with
pack saddle and kyacks but with the top pack omitted and
a burlap pad between the child and the pack ropes. At
the age of 5 or 6 he can ride on a saddle. At 8 or 10 he can
walk much of the time, but a riding donkey should be
available so that he can rest his legs from time to time.
One child at the age of 4 rode behind the saddle on a large
donkey his mother was riding, "holding onto Mother's
balance" as he described it.

Anything else we can think of to suggest would come
under the heading of hints to parents at home or anywhere, and for such advice we refer you to higher author-
ity than ours. (And this even though the contributors have
twenty-six children.) So now if you decide to make parent-
hood a rugged trail instead of a plush-lined job, more
power to you, and may you and the children be the richer
for it.

12. Burro Trips

WHY USE PACK ANIMALS? The answer to this is clear to those who cannot carry even the moderate loads required of the backpacker, or to those who prefer a more varied ration and more comforts than a backpacker dare include in his critical pack. For these people there would be no trip if it were not an animal pack trip. Other reasons are less impelling, but should not be overlooked by those who have never tried pack animals. Each method of mountain travel has disadvantages which are peculiar to itself, and each has rewards which are distinctive. A pack trip not only frees the backpacker of his burden, but also offers many new pleasures of its own.

The donkey is the most desirable beast of burden for the novice, and remains the favorite of many experienced campers. In the West this animal is known by his more colorful Spanish name, "burro." The burro is small and gentle, yet strong and dependable. No pack animal excells him for surefootedness, or matches him for character. He can be packed by school children, but invariably taxes the ingenuity of the adult. No one who is healthy enough and old enough and young enough to go into the mountains at all is barred from a burro trip. It is the trip for the family. It is the trip for the fisherman, or artist, or botanist who has too much gear to carry on his own back. It is also the trip for anyone who wishes to learn to handle pack animals, and the importance of the lesson should not be overlooked by any devotee of the backpack. Having practiced on the small and patient burro, a man can handle the faster mule. If he prefers to let a horse watch the trail and walk in the mule's dust, he can ride. Rock climbers and hunters can use pack animals to establish a base camp which will serve as a center for extended operations. A type of trip which has been called cache-and-carry consists of overnight, or three-day backpack excursions from a succession of base camps, stocked by pack-animal transport. Indeed, the camper who can both hike and pack, can invent many combinations of his own.

Familiarity with the subject matter of the preceding chapters should guarantee the efficiency, safety, and satisfaction of backpack trips. It is the purpose of this chapter to make the few additions and modifications necessary to include the essentials of planning and conducting trips with pack animals.

Personnel and stock

Little prior planning is needed before backpackers can hit the trail. More preparation is advisable before a pack train leaves the corral. What will be the starting point? That may depend upon the availability of pack stock. How many animals will be reserved? To answer this question the pack load must be known, and this in turn depends upon food and equipment lists. These are determined by the length of the trip and the size of the party.

Only those who can carry a pack are invited on a backpack trip. In making up your burro-trip party, select those friends who will lend a hand with the burro management. It is a mistake to relegate all the packing to one or

two men. The stronger backs should lift the loads onto
the saddles, but women can pack as well as men, and the
youngsters can coil ropes and lead the animals on the trail.

To determine the number of animals needed, the approximate pack load must be calculated. The number of
pounds of food to be provided can be determined before
actual purchases are made. If the menu will be that of the
backpacker, 2¼ pounds per man day is a reliable figure;
if it is to include more canned goods, and perhaps a few
fresh foods for special treats, 2¾ pounds per man day is
a better estimate. The weight of personal and community
equipment can be determined in advance by examining
the stuff in the family camp closet in the light of the lists
in the appendix and the discussion below. Allow for a little
extra cooking equipment for the more elaborate cuisine,
and do not underestimate. Add these weights and point off
two decimal places to determine the number of burros required. The stock requirement for a ten-day trip can be
approximated by dividing the number of people by two,
and then taking the nearest larger number of whole burros.
These figures are based upon a 100-pound pay load per
burro, which is maximum. Large donkeys can carry a little
more if well packed, but many are too small or too old or
too tired to carry this much.

It is very difficult to keep more than ten burros together
on the trail. Fewer animals will serve the needs of nearly
every private party, and those who are able to take trips
of more than two weeks' duration should consider the
possibility of touching civilization at some point to restock
provisions. If four men will each carry 25 pounds at the
start of the trip, one animal can be saved, and the back-
packs will reduce rapidly as food is eaten.

Having determined the number of animals needed, you
are ready to order stock. Some packers do not keep bur-

ros because there is more demand for mules, and it is difficult to keep burros with the larger animals. The available donks may be spoken for early in the season; therefore you should make reservations well in advance. If your friends cannot advise you, write to the Park Service or Forest Service and ask for the names and addresses of the packers in the general area of your preference who handle burros. Before making final arrangements with a packer, be sure that he knows just what pack equipment he is expected to supply.

Food and equipment

Campers who use pack animals seldom restrict themselves to the bill-of-fare of the backpacker, or to his abridged equipment list. Why should they? However, a pack trip should still be a go-light trip, and before preparing elaborate menus and an extensive wardrobe you will do well to consider the price, and be sure that you want to drag civilization along with you on what was to have been a camping trip. Additional weight means more burros to be found in the morning, to be loaded and unloaded, and to kick up dust along the trail. That extra pair of pants you are considering would always be at the bottom of your dunnage bag when you wanted them, and would be another item for you to wash, and to pack and unpack daily. Each camper will want to decide for himself what he considers to be a reasonable compromise between necessity and luxury. A few necessities peculiar to pack trips, and several of the luxuries found to be favorites, are pointed out here.

Canned goods are too heavy to be packed in quantity, but a few canned items will break the monotony of rice and spaghetti. Sweetened condensed milk makes several tasty confections, a can of your favorite vegetable may be hoarded for a special occasion, sweet pickles add variety to dry lunches, and jam mixed with snow makes a refreshing sherbet on a climb.

Take a reflecting oven, and plan to do a lot of baking. The ingredients are light and the culinary possibilities are many. Hot buttered biscuits go well in the morning, and how would baked trout do for a change? For the evening meal, why not try cinnamon rolls? or nut cake with chocolate frosting? or an apple cobbler? Build a hot fire against a vertical rock, and prepare a level place for the oven, fairly close to the coals. Keep the reflecting surfaces of the oven shiny and clean. The oven will last longer if it is packed between pieces of plywood held in place by canvas straps.

In selecting personal equipment you have more freedom than the backpacker, but only a few departures from his list are desirable. He considered taking an extra pair of light-weight shoes to wear in camp and probably decided against it; you decide to include them. You can take more moving picture film, and a $\frac{3}{4}$-length air mattress. The backpacker could not decide whether to take a one-man tent or a poncho, so he flipped a coin. You cannot decide either, so you take both. Work gloves are handy about the fire.

Your personal equipment will probably weigh between 18 and 25 pounds and should be packed in a cylindrical dunnage bag. Bulky dunnage is not suitable for burro loads; therefore bags should not be more than 3 feet long and 15 inches in diameter. If your dunnage should be more bulky, or if it should weigh more than 25 pounds, pack it in two dunnage bags, or roll your sleeping bag as a separate bundle. You will want to carry a light knapsack so that your lunch, camera, parka, and band-aids will be readily accessible during the day.

In addition to the usual thongs and pliers, the tool kit should include large split rivets with washers, and some short lengths of leather strap for repairing harness. A coil of light wire and a small can of casein furniture glue are invaluable for repairing a broken saddle. A screwdriver, a tack hammer, and a little box of assorted screws and nails may be useful. Throw in a couple of ax wedges, an extra buckle, and a swivel. A shoemaker's hand awl is excellent for mending torn pack covers, cinches, and canvas kyacks. Fishing line serves as thread. A 50-pound spring scale is convenient for balancing the pairs of kyacks in the morning.

An ax and shovel are useful on pack trips. The ax should have a 26-inch handle and a 2-pound head; the shovel, a 36-inch handle and an 8-inch blade. To render the ax a less formidable weapon, provide a leather ax-head cover.

Your own first-aid materials will be those of any other camper, but to the list in the appendix add some boric acid powder to provide for your burros. (See below.)

The packer will furnish all pack equipment, but it is well to know what this should include so that you can check it over and see that it is all there, and is in good condition. A packer will usually exchange faulty equipment for a camper who knows what he wants. Each burro should have a halter, a lead rope, a saddle and saddle blanket, two kyacks, a pack cover, and a pack rope. In addition, the pack train should have one or two curry combs, and several bells.

Halters must fit snugly. Lead ropes should not be frayed, and should have snap-swivels for attachment to the halter ring. It would be too much to ask for clean saddle blankets, but at least they should not be matted hard, or full of holes. Good blankets are essential for sound backs.

Many good kinds of saddles and harnesses have been

developed for pack animals. The wooden cross-tree or saw-
buck pack saddle may not be the best, but it is good, and
is standard equipment in this country. Cinches should be
broad, clean, and strong. Two cinches are preferable to
one; however the rear cinch is not essential and is not
always supplied. The saddle is usually provided with a
breast strap, as figured on page 108, but a few packers
do not supply them because they claim that a breast strap
which is tight enough to do any good cuts the animal's
wind. This is not quite true. It will cut the wind if the
saddle slips back, but in this event the animal should be
repacked at once. When the saddle is in place, the breast
strap helps to keep it there without discomfort to the
animal.

The harness which goes around the animal's hind quarters is the breech. It is required to keep the pack from
slipping forward. The breech strap should be broad, and
the smaller straps which hold it in place should be strong
and adjustable.

The kyacks—containers which hang from the saddle—
may be made of canvas or of plywood. The latter are
called box kyacks and are just large enough to hold two
five gallon oil cans standing side by side. (Such a can
makes a fine water bucket if the top is cut out and a handle provided.) Most people prefer box kyacks to the more
flimsy canvas ones because they are easier to pack; however, both are satisfactory and one or two pairs of canvas
kyacks are convenient for bulky dunnage. Kyacks are sus-
pended from the cross-trees of the saddle by loops (or
ears) of leather or rope, which should preferably be adjustable.

The pack rope should be at least 30 feet long. Braided
cotton ropes do not kink and are soft to handle when dry,
but twisted ropes are stronger and more durable. Pack

covers are canvas tarpaulins, 5 x 5 feet, or larger. They are more useful in camp if free of holes, and waterproof.

Itinerary

Do not prepare a detailed itinerary in advance; wait and see where the fish are biting, what the weather is like, and how your legs feel. On the other hand do not deny yourself the pleasure of poring over a topographic map to become familiar with place names, and to figure out several desirable alternative routes. Plan to make a loop if you can, so that you will not need to retrace any steps. A burro train can often be taken cross country between two trail nets if the going is not excessively rough; however, the route should be reconnoitered in advance. You will average 8 or 10 miles a day, and should not count on doing more than 12 miles any day, although it is possible to with light loads and an early start. Plan on short hauls for the first few days, and allow time for layover days at the more scenic camps.

To the requisites of a good campsite outlined in an earlier chapter, be sure to add adequate feed for your animals. If firewood is scarce at a desirable campsite use the burros to haul in a good supply.

Before heading up the trail, you will want to call on the district ranger. It is to your advantage that he know where you are going, and you will have many questions to ask. Which passes are open? Are slides, high water, or windfalls obstructing any trails? Is there poison feed along your proposed route? And do not forget a fire permit.

Daily routine

Hit the trail early; the morning is the time to travel. Even the cooks can pack their personal dunnage before breakfast if they take turns at the stirring spoon, and as the cocoa heats, appetites will be sharpened if kyacks are weighed and cans flattened. One person sets out the lunch materials so that all can stow them away into bandannas or pockets, between helpings of mush. A crew goes after the animals as soon as the last trout has been reduced to a skeleton, and those remaining in camp wash dishes, stack the pots, fold the ovens, thoroughly drown the fires, cover the garbage pit, and prepare everything for packing as soon as the burros arrive.

You will probably enjoy taking rather long noon halts when the schedule permits. The warm mid-day sun invites relaxation, and there should be no reason to hurry down the trail again while chewing the last bite of lunch. A quick dip in the river before eating will shorten the miles ahead, and this is a good time for a sun bath. The preparation of lunches in the morning makes it unnecessary to unpack kyacks, and the animals are quickly cared for as described in the next chapter.

Avoid late camps. It is no fun doing the dishes in the dark, and there should be time before supper to bathe and wash clothes, or to fish. When the dishes are washed, pack covers are spread over the kyacks to protect their loads from moisture, and to discourage the little white-footed mouse who loves to nibble holes in food sacks.

There are other animals which are potentially more dangerous to food and equipment than mice. The burros themselves can clean you out of breakfast cereals in short order, and will do so if given the chance. Deer seldom rob the larder, but they are ravenous for salt, and will chew the back out of a shirt, or carry off burro halters for the perspiration they contain. For some reason deer also like soap! In national parks they are often very persistent and difficult to keep away. The bear is the most famous, but in usual experience the least damaging, night marauder.

Bears are not common above 8,000 feet, but they often investigate camps. When in bear country, put plates and cups on top of the pack covers which are covering the kyacks. If you hear a clatter during the night, collect your wits for a moment, and then suddenly jump up, turn on your flashlight, shout, and throw a pine cone at the re- treating (you hope) robber. A bear is not to be fooled with at close range, but this method has worked many times, and the culprits seldom return for a second treat- ment. This method can also very effectively startle any member of your party who stumbles into it.

Pack animals add many routine jobs to the daily schedule. You will find that most of these chores are fun, but you can increase your pleasure in doing them by striv- ing constantly to increase your skill. If the party divides itself into teams to pack the burros, have each team criti- cize the jobs done by the others. Time yourselves making and breaking camp, and be on the lookout for shortcuts and improvements in technique. Since you have more equipment than the backpacker, your camp should be more orderly. You cannot get along if a pack rope is lost, but there is no danger of losing it if it is always kept in the appointed place. Before leaving a campsite, look for any article of equipment which may have been overlooked in packing, check the area for papers which should have been burned, be sure the garbage pit is well covered (and uninviting to bears), and that the fire bed is cool. It is a regrettable fact that it is possible to leave many favorite campsites *cleaner* than you find them. If you will carry your burned and flattened cans out with you—thus avoid- ing the need of a garbage pit for unburnables—you'll be one of the best friends of the wilderness.

13. Burro Management

BURRO MANAGEMENT is the uncertain science of getting a burro to do what one wants him to do. Now if he were a frail animal he might be forced into submission by strong-arm methods; but he is stronger than a man. If he were a beast of no individuality, he might do his packer's bidding without question; but he is quite opinionated about a number of things. How, then, can one hope to manage him? The answer is simple, he can be managed by any camper who is more intelligent than he. Are you? Face the question squarely.

If so, then instead of waging constant war against him, you solicit his cooperation. A burro is more responsive than a mule and will be quick to detect and return friendship; the bray of affection with which he greets his packer in the morning is as heartwarming as it is ear-rending. The camper should realize that his beast of burden is working hard for him, doing a job he could not do himself. Certainly the animal deserves to be well packed, well fed, and well rested. He may become angry or resentful but he is not irrevocably mean; if you find him ornery, you have his previous handler to thank. Realize that he does certain things in certain ways because he is pure burro. It is nevertheless important that the animal know who is in charge. Do not give in to him on important disciplinary matters. He will object at first but will respect your strength of character and admire you secretly. An attitude of firmness, coupled with consideration, is of paramount importance as a background for good burro management; the rest is technique and experience.

The technique is not difficult to learn and with surprisingly little experience the novice becomes an expert packer, confident of his ability to cope with any problem the next turn in the trail may present and deriving much real satisfaction from his mastery of a new skill.

Finding them in the morning

Let us consider the tricks of getting a burro to do what we want him to do by talking ourselves through a typical day, considering the problems as they come. If the animals were picketed last night, we know just where to look for them. If they were turned loose, finding them becomes the first problem of the day. Some campers never got beyond this first problem, but such a fate should seldom be blamed entirely on bad luck. It never pays merely to wander about listening for burro bells. After breakfast all members of the party except dishwashers join forces for a coordinated, calculated search. There are two methods: one is to start at camp and track the animals; the other, which may be faster but which is less reliable, is to guess where they are and go directly there. It is usually well to do both these things at once. Spread out and go where you would have gone if you were burros, but keep a sharp lookout for tracks in case your imagination is not quite up to it. The burros did not go to a near-by meadow of tall lush grass, because they prefer the bunchgrass which grows on higher ground. They spent the first part of the night finding and eating such grass. When appetites were satisfied, they probably just stood still. Bells may even now be quiet. In the early morning they may have climbed the west wall of the canyon to meet the sun as it descended the slopes. When they reached it, they probably stood again and warmed themselves. If you were slow at breakfast, they are again moving on and feeding. Wherever they are, you may expect to find them together unless there is reason to suppose that certain of the animals have developed friendships bordering on love. Half an hour will usually serve to find your stock.

If there are two or three burros, it is best to lead them back to camp with the lead ropes which you have brought with you. If there are more animals and few hands it may be preferable to drive them. They will be easier to catch upon arrival in camp if they are not unnecessarily excited. They are frisky in the morning and may run down the trail, but this should not be encouraged, and one should avoid swinging ropes and shouting. Party members left in camp have learned to spread out across the trail when they hear the bells so that the animals will not go on past camp. The next problem is to catch them.

Catching them

Your burros may be so friendly that you have trouble keeping them out of your lunch pocket, or, on the other hand, they may be very difficult to approach. Catch the gentle ones first and then go after that suspicious creature who seems to be paying little attention to the good example set by the others. If several campers stand about the recalcitrant beast at various places it will help by forming a mental corral. Do not carry a rope. Hold one hand out and talk to the animal quietly. Mother Goose will do if you cannot think of anything more appropriate. Approach very slowly. Pretend that you do not care much whether you catch him or not. If the burro bolts the circle, do not run after him but start the process all over. If he thinks this is fun, wait until the other burros have been saddled and he may decide the game is done. As a last resort, put a level teaspoon of quick oats in the palm of your hand and do it all again. When your arm is around the animal's neck, an assistant comes up slowly with a lead rope, and a halter, if the burro is not already wearing one. He will be easier to catch in another day or two.

Tying them up

Even the gentlest burro must be tied before packing operations begin. He might stand still for nine mornings but on the tenth he may suddenly give in to an impelling urge to run just as the load is about to be secured. We have seen campers stand with pack rope in hand watching the pack cover sail into the fire place, the eating utensils ricochet through a willow thicket, and the flour sack explode on a distant rock as the burro disappears over the horizon.

Tie them to small, stout trees near the dunnage, and not too close to each other. The lead rope is secured to the tree at least waist high, and the rope should be short. This discourages the burro from walking round and round the tree as you follow with the saddle and prevents him from stepping over the rope or becoming tangled in rocks or brush.

This brings us to the subject of knots which calls for a short digression. Every camper should know the following knots: square knot, bowline, sheet bend, clove hitch, and two half hitches. Packers must also know the girth hitch. These are enough for every-day needs. Old hands will also find uses for the hitching tie, magnus hitch, eye splice, short splice, timber hitch, and others which may

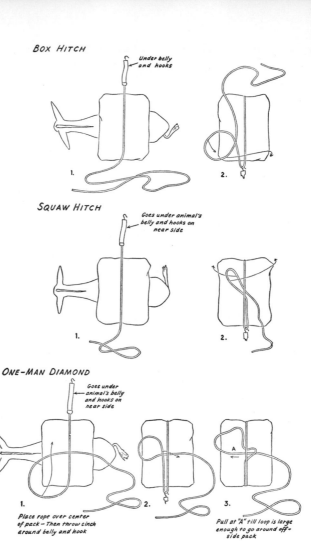

Box Hitch

Under belly and hooks

1.

2.

Squaw Hitch

Goes under animal's belly and hooks on near side

1.

2.

One-Man Diamond

Goes under animal's belly and hooks on near side

1.

Place rope over center of pack — Then throw cinch around belly and hook

2.

3.

A

Pull at "A" till loop is large enough to go around off-side pack

3.

Secure to
cinch ring

4.

3.

4.

4.

5.

6.

*Make loop "B", then pull at "C" to
lock "B"—Now place loop "A" and
tighten, starting at rear.*

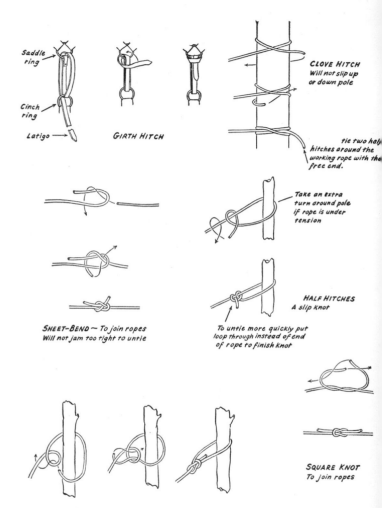

Saddle ring

Cinch ring

Latigo

GIRTH HITCH

CLOVE HITCH
Will not slip up
or down pole

tie two half
hitches around the
working rope with the
free end.

Take an extra
turn around pole
if rope is under
tension

SHEET-BEND — To join ropes
Will not jam too tight to untie

HALF HITCHES
A slip knot

To untie more quickly put
loop through instead of end
of rope to finish knot

SQUARE KNOT
To join ropes

BOWLINE — For a loop that will not slip

be found in any book of handcraft. We find other people's written directions for knot tying as illuminating as an account of the mechanics of an adding machine, so we are offering only diagrams. One should practice until the essential knots can be tied quickly and easily and should learn the characteristics and uses of each. The *square knot* is the knot usually used for joining two ropes together and for bandaging. The *bowline* is used for making a loop which will not slip. The *sheet bend,* like the square knot, is used for joining two ropes—particularly when they are of different sizes, but unlike the square knot it can be untied easily after it has been under strain. The *clove hitch* will not slip up or down a smooth pole or stick. Two *half hitches* can be tied in a rope which is under strain and is usually good for tying a lead rope to that certain small tree standing alone on level ground—which brings us back to that subject again.

Grooming

The burro is now ready for grooming, an important step which is too often overlooked. His back should get a good working over with a curry comb to remove dirt, salt, and sand. The legs should be kept free of caked mud, but otherwise little additional grooming is needed.

Until you learn which animals are appreciative and you have established a mutual understanding with any others, it is well to remember that one end may bite and the other end may kick. The bite is most often a feint and seldom more than a nip; the kick is not as damaging as a mule kick, but it is foolish to take chances. To keep posted on the disposition of a particular horse, mule, or burro, one should keep an eye on his ears. He will take no aggressive action with malice aforethought without turning his ears back along his neck—farther back than when just listening to the rear. The first time he nips at you is the test. Thump him solidly in the ribs and talk to him. Billingsgate is better than Mother Goose this time. This establishes that mutual understanding we spoke of and he probably will not trouble you again.

If there is a saddle or cinch sore, every effort must be made to avoid further irritation. The harness may require adjustment. The load should be redistributed among the sound animals if possible. Remove dirt with a clean rag, avoid excessive dust and prevent the animal from rolling. Clean soft saddle blankets are desirable for prevention as well as for cure. Dirty ones may be rinsed out on layover days with great benefit to the animals' backs. There are saddle-sore creams and greases on the market and many packers have their own formulas. Most of these sound like witches' brews. You might carry a little boric acid powder to sprinkle on sores. This is a mild antiseptic and helps dry up open wounds. Clean air and sunshine are best. Good packers do not treat sores; they prevent them.

Saddling

Saddling and packing are done from the near (left) side of the animal. It is a good idea to work in pairs, but the off-side packer acts only as an assistant, doing the things which cannot be done on the near side. The animal has learned to expect this, and the routine helps the packers also. Make sure the saddle blanket is free of wrinkles and burrs. Place it too far forward and slide it back into position so that the animal's hair will lie smooth. The front margin comes to the center of the withers. Some burros have a convenient dark stripe at this point to guide the novice. If the blanket is too far to one side it will creep out from under the saddle during the morning. Stand behind the burro—not too close—and check.

Swashbuckling cowboys like to throw on the saddle so that the cinches slap the animal in the belly. This is bad practice for any packer and is very bad practice for the beginner. Lift the cinch back over the saddle to get it out of the way and then place the saddle on the animal's back. It fits in the hollows just behind the withers—not too far back. Push the cinch down the off side, buckle the breast strap, if the saddle has one, and drop the breech harness over the animal's—well, breech. The saddle blanket should extend forward at least two and a half inches beyond the saddle where the latter rests on the back. This is important. Now grasp the saddle blanket front and back along the animal's ridge pole and lift an inch or so; this makes a tunnel of air under the blanket in the midline which provides ventilation and prevents the load from rubbing along the backbone.

The long strap used to secure the cinch is called the latigo. The off-side packer pushes the cinch under the belly to the near-side packer, who passes the latigo through the cinch ring from inside out and then continues through the ring on the saddle rigging from outside in. This is repeated to give two complete loops with the latigo, the second loop being over the first, in the rings, rather than beside it. The forward edge of the cinch must be not less than three inches from the front leg when the animal stands straight so that it will not pinch when he walks. Cinch sores behind the leg are very difficult to heal. The loops made with the latigo provide enough friction to hold as the cinch is tightened. In anticipation of this event, the burro has spread his legs and lowered his head. His lip is dangling and he is looking as sullen as he can. Most important, he may have taken an enormous breath which he does not plan to exhale until you think that the cinch is tight. Pay no attention to this. Put the left hand against the body of the animal beside the cinch ring to prevent the skin from wrinkling. With the right hand, grasp the outside loop of the latigo between the two rings and give several good hard pulls. Secure the latigo with the girth hitch. The poor burro is now moaning and grunting and eyeing you reproachfully, but never mind, in two minutes the cinch will be hanging free. Saddle another burro and then come back in a casual sort of way, humming a little tune, and quickly tighten the cinch again before the beast can inflate. This time test it by passing the fingers under the cinch from back to front. They should go all the way under but with some difficulty. When the fingers are withdrawn they smooth the hair.

If there is a rear cinch, it is placed after the front cinch. It goes just behind the "equator," and must not be so tight as the front cinch. If it is too tight, the animal cannot breathe well. There should be a strap between the breeching and the rear cinch to be snapped in place. When pulling the animal's tail out from under the breech strap so that he can have the benefit of its services, stand at the burro's left flank with the left hand on his hip and with arm straight. A burro can kick front and back but not far to the side. This position is safe until he changes his stance, and the arm gives quick notice of such a tactic. If the animal should object, give up the project. He may be able to free his tail himself and if not he will repent the first time a horse fly comes along.

Packing

The load a burro can carry and the characteristics of kyacks were discussed in chapter 12. It is essential that the load be balanced for both weight and bulk. The kyacks should be within three pounds of each other. The off-side packer lifts his kyack first, because it is more convenient

to remove this kyack last when unpacking the animal without assistance. The near-side packer loops the ears of this
kyack over the cross-trees of the saddle and then lifts his
kyack. The ears are placed and both kyacks are eased down
at once so that the saddle will not be pulled to one side.
Canvas kyacks are loaded so that the member of the pair
provided with the strap is on the off side. This strap is
secured to the buckle of the near-side kyack. Stand behind
to see that the load is balanced at this stage. If the saddle
has been pulled to one side, recheck the weights of the
kyacks. If the saddle is straight but one kyack is lower
than the other, correct the lengths of the ear loops. If the
loops are not adjustable, rematch all kyacks to obtain
more suitable pairs.

Now comes the top load. Miscellaneous, odd-shaped
items are not in order. Compact bedding rolls or dunnage bags are fine. See page 112 regarding dimensions. A
single bedding roll goes crosswise between the cross-trees
of the saddle. If two rolls are used, they go lengthwise, one
resting on top of each kyack. Check the balance of the
load again and then spread the pack cover over the top.
Tuck the corners in so that they will not flap. If the cross
trees can be left exposed, it will be easier for you to see
the position of the saddle during the morning.

At first it is easiest for two campers to work together in
throwing the pack hitch, but after gaining experience one
may prefer to do it alone. The hitches diagrammed can
all be tightened as they are thrown and should be made
just as tight as possible. The tension is all on the pack and
does not bother the animal. One good pack hitch will serve
the needs of most campers but there is satisfaction in
knowing several. It is suggested that the beginner learn
the three hitches diagrammed here in the order given: The
squaw hitch is a very good general purpose hitch, which

is easily learned and rapidly thrown and untied. It uses a minimum of rope. It is best suited to compact or high loads. The *one-man diamond hitch* is the favorite of most experienced packers. It is more difficult to learn but makes a very tight and neat pack; with practice it is quickly thrown and untied. The *box hitch* uses only a little more rope. It is best suited to broad flat loads. Fishing rod cases, camera tripod and the ax go on last. They are stuck under the pack ropes at the top of the pack.

Now that the hitch has been thrown, stand back and gaze on your handiwork. It probably looks like a cumulus cloud or an erupting volcano—they usually do at first—but do not repack it if the saddle is still straight. There is a reasonable chance that it will stay on until noon and you will do much better after lunch.

On the trail

It is advisable to lead each burro during the first and last days and whenever the trail is rough. It is essential that enough campers walk with the pack train to give each animal prompt attention if the trail becomes muddy, or a pack slips, or the party must pass a column of mules. Indeed, the sudden whim of a single animal may necessitate the supervision of all. The animals may be allowed to run free when circumstances permit, but they should be kept together. The lead rope is then secured to the top of the pack. It should be loose enough so the animal can just reach water to drink. If there is more slack, he will step over the rope and become entangled.

Burros set a pace which is very good for family groups but which may seem slow to some people. As long as the pack train keeps moving, there is little to do about it but accept gracefully the fact that a burro cannot be made to hurry. Trail burners who have thought of some reason for hurrying past the scenes they came to enjoy should not walk with burros. However, at times the pack train may slow down to a pace which is unreasonable—even for donkeys. One man should then walk behind each burro —particularly if they are being led. A burro can pull against the tug of a lead rope and can watch the man who holds it. He is apprehensive about a man behind him who offers no weight he can resist. This apprehension is increased if the pesky man carries a willow switch even though he never uses it. Psychology may be used further upon an animal that is slower than the rest. At the head of the pack train, he will retard the entire party unless the burro behind him is impatient and butts him constantly. At the tail of the pack train, he will show his gregarious nature by hurrying to keep up. It is a mistake to shout at the animals or threaten them constantly. This makes them distrustful and skittish.

Try to keep the pack train moving. If a short halt is necessary, hold the animals so that they will not bunch and mill around, or start to graze or wander off. It is very uncomfortable to support a pack when standing still—as any backpacker knows—and burros may become tired and lie down with their loads. This often necessitates repacking. On the other hand the burros may be allowed to stop for short blows on the switchbacks leading up to a pass. Grazing along the trail should be permitted only for such animals as have learned to snatch a bite here and there without stopping. The animals must not be permitted to run. It takes a good pack job to hold together under this treatment, besides the pots and cups make an alarming racket and sugar will not taste good if mixed with salt.

Every member of the party must be on the lookout for shifting loads. This should become second nature. Is the cinch too tight? or too loose? or too far forward? Has the saddle slipped back? or to one side? Has the blanket crept out from under the saddle? The rest of the load is less important so long as it hangs together. Particular vigilance is required on downhill stretches. If a load slips, it should be repacked at the first suitable place in the trail or sores will result. It may be best to stop the entire pack train. In any event, one animal should not be taken from a train alone; he will be too restless to stand quietly.

Horses and mules should not drink if overheated from hard work, but burros may nearly always be allowed to drink as often and as much as they want.

Fording streams.

In general, burros can ford any stream a man can cross without swimming. If there is a current, the water must not be deep enough to strike the animal's belly. The difficulty of the ford increases with the roughness of the river bed, although animals prefer large cobbles to soft sand or mud. Some burros will enter a swift stream without even pausing at the bank, and others require considerable persuasion. Psychology may help considerably. If the willing animals and most of the personnel cross first, and go a short distance up the trail, the remaining donks will at least see that they cannot persuade the party to turn back. A gentle entry should be sought, which is not muddy and where the water is quiet enough so that the bottom can be seen. Now if several campers stand behind to cut off retreat, a few good whacks with a stick on the burro's dry-land end will usually send him on his way. If the first try is not successful, the fifth may bring results, therefore one should not give up. However, if there is sufficient manpower in the party, time can be saved by pushing and dragging the animal into the water. Once his feet are wet he will keep going. If the stream is swift and the load heavy, the smaller animals should be escorted across. One of us once watched a burro capsize in mid-stream and slowly submerge a kyack containing a large sack of sugar. The poor animal could not get up and the pack bubbled merrily as we waded to the rescue. A lot of potential hotcake syrup could have been saved had the animal been guided through the water. To do so, one packer should wade on each side of the burro, steadying the kyacks. The animal should be allowed to take his time and will usually do best if he picks his own route. But not always.

The noon halt

As explained in chapter 12, burro trippers usually provide themselves with lunch materials before packing in the morning so that the pack loads do not need to be disturbed at mid-day. It does not follow that the burros do not need to be unpacked. They have been doing all the work and will appreciate the rest. They should be tied in the shade, far enough apart so that each has a separate sphere of influence. Lead ropes are again tied high and fairly short. The pack rope is removed and kyacks and dunnage placed on the ground out of the animals' reach. The pack cover may be spread to protect the load from sun and dust. The cinches should be loosened but not released, because saddles can be left on the animals to speed repacking after lunch, unless it seems advisable to check for sore backs. Saddle blankets should be lifted under the cross-trees of the saddle again as in the morning so animals' backs will cool better.

Mud, snow, and rocks

Mud can be very troublesome. Burros have good reason for their fear of swampy places. Small hoofs do not give much support when under a load. In spite of all efforts to keep away from bogs, an animal may become mired now and then. His struggles cause him to sink deeper and all legs may go out of sight as he rests on his side or belly. He will be trembling with fear and out of breath. Move slowly and talk to him to quiet him. Remove the pack, cutting ropes if necessary, and loosen the cinch. If he is still unable to get up, assist him by pulling on saddle and tail, but be careful of flying hoofs because he will pop out like a cork when he comes. He should not be re-packed until he has recovered his composure.

Burros dislike snow but can cross safely if the snow is not too soft and if a trail is prepared for them. The shovel should be used to dig a path which is as level as possible. Broad steps will help prevent slipping on steep places. Particular care should be taken to fill holes. Stamping with boots and tamping with poles will make the trail solid. The animals should be taken over the bad places one at a time and should always be attended. It is often possible to improvise trails around small snow patches to which the animals have objection. Schedules should be arranged so that passes are crossed early in the day before snow fields have softened in the sun.

Burros are very sure footed. They dance their hoofs from rock to rock with surprising skill and may be trusted to cross any stretch of rough trail which they undertake willingly. If the going is unusually bad, they may need encouragement. Assistance over an obstacle may be given by lifting on the pack, but campers must be careful to avoid being crushed between kyacks and unyielding granite boulders. Where slides or washes have obliterated the trail and detours cannot be found, the animals should be unpacked and their loads hand-carried across.

In the unhappy event that an animal breaks a leg, it should be killed. In the absence of firearms, this is done by striking several hard blows on its temple with an ax. The body should be carried off the trail and buried.

Stubbornness

The notorious stubbornness of a donkey usually reflects an unhappy past. We have never known of a strong healthy burro whose stubbornness could not be overcome in a week by good handling, and one day is often enough. First of all, the animal should not be blamed for physical handicaps or for the faults of his packer. If he is "stubborn" while climbing a pass, his rear cinch may be too tight; if he is "stubborn" descending the other side, he may have stiff shoulders; if he is "stubborn" on the level, he may be overloaded. In our experience most so-called stubbornness is confined to the smaller and weaker burros and may be attributed to fatigue and old age. When such animals cannot be refused at the packer's corral, they should be favored with light loads.

Stubbornness may be the result of fear. This is overcome by not requiring the animal to do anything he cannot do with reasonable safety. Refusal to cross a river at a bad ford shows good judgment, not bad temperament. It is well to remember that few campers can be as familiar with the trail as are the animals they pack.

Stubbornness may also be an attempt on the part of the burro to see what he can get away with. If he learns quickly that he cannot get away with anything unreasonable, he becomes his packer's friend. When confronted with an obdurate animal, give him the benefit of the doubt. See that his pack is in good adjustment and that he is not lame. Be sure that he knows what is expected of him and try arbitration once more. No results. Now do not give him the pleasure of watching you slowly lose your temper as you barrage his long ears with invectives and his tough hide with sticks. Do not use a lip twitch or other instrument of torture. Order him to do your bidding in the tones a battalion commander must use to drill his men, and simultaneously deliver several solid whacks.

This scene should not be long continued, however, and if results are not soon forthcoming, other methods are required. The combined strength of several men is enough literally to drag a burro for a short distance. Two women were forced to change the entire itinerary of their projected summer outing because their one burro refused to cross a certain bridge the first day. When we brought the same burro to the same bridge later in the summer, we could appreciate the girls' plight—this was a fine large strong burro. He spread his legs in the trail and felt and looked quite invincible. However, we got a short, heavy pole and placed it under his rump. With two men on each side we lifted the animal's rear end off the ground and pushed gently forward. Like a wheelbarrow, he started over the bridge on two legs. That burro was brought to that same bridge four more times that season and he did not so much as break a stride. He just looked up at us from under a hairy ear and winked.

Unpacking

When the pack train files into the new campsite in the afternoon, the layout of the camp should be determined quickly so that the animals can be kept out of the kitchen and living room and so that the kyacks can be placed in the pantry as they come off the saddles. There is no trick to unpacking; the job can be done very quickly. The important thing is to dispose of all equipment properly. Pack ropes are coiled and placed together at the base of a tree which is to serve as tool shed. The ax and shovel go here. Pack covers are folded and stacked. The kyacks are lined up together where they will be convenient to the cook, but they ought to remain in pairs because they are matched for corresponding length of ear loops and because some will not be unpacked very much and balance can be maintained for morning packing. Saddles are lined up along a log, if one is available, or on the ground. They may be of different sizes and have been selected to fit certain burros; therefore the names or numbers of the animals should be marked on them to facilitate correct matching in the morning. Each blanket is spread over its respective saddle, animal side out, to dry. If it is threatening rain, the saddles may be stacked and the pile protected with a pack cover. The best way to lose lead ropes is to leave them where the burros were tied before the animals were disposed of for the night. The ropes are collected and are hung over a low limb of the tool shed.

At night

Burros are seldom trained to use hobbles and would be severely cut if hobbled when not accustomed to it. They are picketed or simply turned loose. Picketing is less satisfactory for the burro, is harder on the meadows, and is more trouble at night. Turning the animals free is more trouble in the morning. A single burro is more prone to wander than a social group. Picketing may be desirable the first and last nights to keep within bounds any incipient homesickness for the easy life of the corral. It may save a long search in the morning if the terrain is rather flat so that the animals can wander in any direction. This is particularly true when feed near camp is not of the best. Animals should also be picketed if it is known that there is poison feed in the area. In the West there is a plant known as Death Camas (*Zygadenus venenosus*) which is quickly fatal. It is a member of the lily family, with an inconspicuous whitish flower which grows to a height of about two feet in wet shady meadows. Fortunately burros are in no danger if there is enough bunchgrass for them elsewhere.

Burros must never be tethered unless a suitable area can be found where feed is adequate and the ground is free of rocks or other rope entanglers. Damage to vegetation is great if shoots are young and tender or if the ground is wet.

Since burros stay together, it is sufficient to picket only half of them. If it has been noticed that certain of the string are considered the life of the party by their associates, these are the animals to tie up. From an equine point of view, it is often the jennies which are so regarded. At least one of the picketed animals should have a bell, if available; the familiar sound attracts the others. Offer water if a stream was not crossed late in the day.

Drive a good stake—it will be called upon to take considerable strain and a little piece of rotten wood will not hold. Saplings which are strong enough seldom stand alone and trimming would be required anyway, so it is usually best to cut a stake. A few packers provide light picket chains but the pack rope usually has to serve as tether rope. Tie it to the stake at ground level with a clove hitch; other knots could be pulled off the top of the stake. To be sure that the burro will not wind the knot to the end of the rope and thus be released, it is desirable to tie two half hitches around the running rope (the long end) with the standing rope (the short end). This is always a good way to finish off a clove hitch. The pack rope of an animal which is not to be tied up can be added to the first rope to increase the grazing radius provided that the larger area will be free of ground obstacles. The ropes are joined with a sheet bend. If a square knot were used, it could not be untied in the morning after dew and donkey had conspired to make it tight. The tether rope is now tied to the halter ring with a bowline, or a lead rope is added if it has a snap and swivel. A swivel is very desirable. Burros often walk up and down during the night to keep warm and may completely unwind a twisted rope if no swivel is provided. On unusually cold nights, a blanket held in place by a loosely cinched saddle will help keep a tethered animal warm. It is advisable to check before turning in for the night to see that ropes are free and all is well. On layover days the position of the stakes must be changed as often as needed to assure adequate feed, and water is offered morning and afternoon.

When animals are turned loose for the night, the bells go on the more influential animals. Bell straps are tied tight enough so that they remain under the chin, where they constrict the windpipe less than lower on the neck. The animals might step through loose halters while grazing; therefore they are removed unless they fit snugly. In canyons, pack stock is invariably turned upstream. The animals usually prefer this direction, knowing that feed tends to be better in the more open upper reaches of a mountain watershed. The camper prefers it because the walls of the canyon and the pass beyond form a natural corral within which to seek his stock in the morning. They often leave the flat canyon floor but will not cross the pass unless it is to follow a passing pack train. Burros are rarely guilty of this misdemeanor, but the same cannot be said for single horses and mules.

The National Park Service and Forest Service have constructed drift fences across many canyons. Burro packer and backpacker alike must cooperate in keeping drift fence gates closed. One's faith in his fellow man takes a severe jolt after tracking his stock to a drift fence gate left open by a careless camper.

Horses and mules

Success with a burro is a desirable prerequisite for handling stronger and faster stock.

Good pack horses and mules can carry a pay load of 200 pounds when expertly packed. One hundred and seventy-five pounds should be considered a maximum load on one's first trip. The pack train can be counted on for 15 miles a day on good trails if it keeps pushing. These animals walk at a good clip and, unless their handlers are fast hikers, all personnel should be mounted. This becomes more important as the size of the party increases. Mules are led singly by pedestrians or are tied in groups of not more than five animals and are then led by a man on horseback. This is the "string" of the professional packer. Each lead rope passes through the left hand breech ring of the preceding animal's harness and is then tied around that animal's neck with a bowline. This arrangement keeps the string in control without straining the packs but is risky in rough terrain where one shying mule may roll an entire string.

One or more horses are nearly always sent out with pack mules. The mules, which would otherwise wander far and sometimes independently, are attracted to their animal chaperones and need not be tied up at night. Horses can only be tethered where feed is particularly good and are usually belled and hobbled. It is well not to underestimate the distance a hobbled horse can cover in the night if poor feed and lack of company make travel attractive. Grain is often carried to make capture easier. To facilitate packing, tie the animals to a picket line—a packrope strung shoulder-high between trees. Tie lead ropes with a magnus hitch and they won't slip along the line.

No respectable packer would give a novice a mean or ornery mule to take on a private trip. The greater danger is that an old or ailing animal will be offered. Experienced trail animals are not likely to kick or bite if not provoked; however, the kick of a mule can break a leg. Mules need firmer handling than burros. The best of them give more dependable service.

Burros usually go barefoot, but horses and mules are shod, a slight disadvantage on smooth rock. This is a drawback to the private packer, because shoes may be thrown on an extended trip and prompt reshoeing is desirable, and sometimes necessary before the hoofs go lame or become so worn that a new shoe cannot be fitted. Extra shoes for front and rear should be carried on a trip of more than a week's duration because one often chances to pass professional packers who are otherwise equipped to replace a worn shoe.

The longer legs and greater strength of horses and mules make water, snow, and mud less formidable obstacles. Greater ability is coupled with greater willingness. Larger hoofs in proportion to weight give horses an advantage and they should precede over snowfields and bogs.

Whether you use the mule or either of his parents, we urge that you duly consider the welfare of meadows, the limiting factor in mountain usage for those traveling with stock. Fewer flowers nod to lazy breezes in overgrazed meadows; grass does not seed itself adequately and the luxuriance of a natural garden has been impaired for the next season; further trampling of grassy slopes leads to erosion and the permanent loss to generations of mountain lovers of pasture which might have supported the stock which could have carried their sleeping bags, cameras, and fishing rods to vacation spots now denied them because campers who went before them did not look ahead.

14. Wilderness Prospect

THERE YOU HAVE IT—the story of what you can do along the sky-land trails of the wilderness. We should like to think there is enough scope and persuasion in what has been said here to speed you on your way to the nearest roadhead, there to pocket your car key for a few weeks and see what lies beyond. If there isn't enough scope and persuasion, we'd appreciate knowing—for future editions.

Our indirect purpose in this book, as we said, is to encourage you to learn enough about the wilderness to feel a real stake in preserving it, not only for today's travelers, but also for the unnumbered who are entitled to explore and enjoy wild lands as pleasant as ours. There ought always to be a wide, beautiful, natural world—in places. There always will be so long as man handles his scenic treasures with care and guards them against the threat that stems from his own prodigality.

May there be many to stand watch among those who learn the pleasures of going light!

APPENDIX

Appendix: Food Lists

WE GIVE HERE two varieties of food lists—the first rather general, to provide an approximate guide to items in various categories, with a fairly liberal range of amounts; the second quite specific, listing the exact amounts of each item used in a 100-man-day, two-week trip by a mixed group. The lists differ greatly.

The second list provides no margin for extended periods of cold weather or for an unusual number of layover days; either of these factors would increase the food required, as would an emergency which prevented a party's getting out of the mountains on schedule—or an accidental loss of food owing to weather, gravity, wildlife, or cooking tragedy.

It is the general experience that the real mountain appetite does not build up until about the tenth day of a trip, after which the amount of food consumed is prodigious. Age is of course an important factor; a group of growing boys can upset an otherwise well-planned food list. If the party is young, traveling far and high in cool places, and out for a month or more, the per-man-day figure should probably be two and a half pounds.

1. *General food requirements* (in pounds per man-day)

Starches (precook where possible), 0.45–0.60

> Dry cereal (if the bulk is deemed worth while); oatmeal; cream of wheat or wheat flakes; yellow corn meal; concentrated dried soups; soy, pea, or bean flour (for soups); spaghetti, noodles, or macaroni; dried potatoes (preferably precooked,—so-called

[144]

"Instant"); rice (preferably instant; brown if cooking time permits); rye crackers, hardtack, hard crackers, etc.; pancake flour, or white flour and baking powder; dried peas, lentils, beans (precooked).

Sugars, 0.35–0.45

White sugar (use liberally); brown or raw sugar (makes better syrup); candies (hard candies digested sooner than chocolate).

Nuts (shelled and salted), 0.10–0.15

Walnuts, almonds, peanuts, cashews, brazils, etc.

Dried fruits and vegetables, 0.30–0.45

Apples, apricots, peaches, pears, figs, raisins, dates (don't take sticky kinds) prunes, carrots, beets, tomatoes (dried or canned paste), onions, etc. Tomatoes and onions valuable for flavoring.

Fats and fatty foods, 0.10–0.15

Butter or margarine (put in nearly everything; soups, mush, noodles, vegetables, etc.); bacon (put fat in mush, soup, etc.); peanut butter.

Protein, 0.40–0.60

Canadian bacon, dried beef, ham, spam, etc.; salami, corned beef (this is heavy), liverwurst; whole milk powder (use in nearly everything); mild cheese; powdered whole egg.

Beverage materials, to suit

Coffee, tea, cocoa, bouillon cubes, jello (for hot drinks), orange or lemon powder.

Flavoring materials, to suit

Salt (use generously), pepper, onion salt, celery salt, cinnamon, maple flavor, chili powder plus any others in your repertoire.

Total food per man-day, 2.00–2.50.

A few pointers until you ascertain your own preferences:

1. You will probably want to eat your starches roughly as follows: 30 per cent at breakfast, 30 at lunch, and 40 at dinner.

2. Your protein should probably include 0.12 to 0.17 pounds per man-day of milk powder, and 0.05 to 0.15 pounds of cheese.

3. Take at least 0.015 pounds per man-day of salt, and don't spill it or drop it in the creek.

List for 100 man-days (in pounds per item for period)

Beverage
  Hemo   5.0
  Tea (96 bags)   .6
  Instant coffee   1.0
Breads
  Wheat thins, trisket   1.8
  Pumpernickel, Swiss rye   5.0
  Fig, apricot newtons   4.7
Candy
  Caramels (wrapped)   4.1
  Chocolate   6.2
  Hard (wrapped)   7.7
Cereal
  Cornmeal, wheatmeal   3.5
  Oatmeal, quick   3.5
  Pancake flour   3.0
Cheese
  Cheddar, Jack, Swiss   10.3
Condiments
  Salt   0.6
  Onion flakes   0.6
  Tomato flakes   0.6
  Lemons (2)   0.3
  Chili, garlic powders,
    cinnamon   0.1
Desserts
  Jello   1.1
  Instant butterscotch,
    tapioca, and vanilla
    puddings   5.1
Dried fruit
  Apple nuggets   1.7
  Banana flakes   0.6
  Apricots, peaches   10.5
  Dates (pitted), figs,
    raisins   8.0

  Prunes   6.5
Dried milk   8.7
Butter or oleo   3.5
Nuts—peanuts and mixed   8.2
Protein
  Bacon (Canadian)   3.5
  Corned beef   5.0
  Dried Beef   1.0
  Dried egg   1.2
  Ham (canned), spam   5.0
  Salami, Italian   3.5
  Tuna, canned chicken   5.0
Soups, dried
  Bouillon cubes   0.8
  Split pea, onion,
    chicken   2.8
Starch
  Macaroni   1.2
  Noodles   2.6
  Potatoes, powdered   2.4
  Rice   1.1
  Spaghetti   2.4
Sugar
  Brown   3.5
  White   7.0
Miscellaneous items
  Vitamin C, 50 mg. tab-
    lets (200)
  Soap (0.5 bar)
  Toilet paper (5 rolls)
  Matches (large box)
  SOS pads (1 box),
    scouring cloths   1.0
    Total   161.5

Comments

This list provides a fair variety within skeleton menus for each meal: *Breakfast*—stewed fruit, cooked cereal, bacon, Hemo, and occasionally pancakes or scrambled eggs. *Lunch*—cheese, dried fruits, nuts, chocolate or caramels, salami, whole-grain breadstuff. *Dinner*—soup, a gow dish, dessert, and tea. The composition of gow depends on the bravery and ingenuity of the cook.

The larger the group, the greater the ease of variation and the less important the consideration of individual dislikes, for someone else is bound to compensate for that peculiarity. (However, one shouldn't let his eating education stop at the three-year level!)

The average daily intake from the suggested food list compares adequately, for moderately active men and women, with the recommended daily allowances (1948 revision) set up by the Food and Nutrition Board of the National Research Council, except for vitamin C. Lemon and orange concentrates supply significant quantities of this vitamin.

A few of the items listed are particularly valuable in this diet in the amounts allotted. They are: dried apricots and peaches, milk, ham, corned beef, cheese, nuts and Hemo, a chocolate drink fortified with vitamins and minerals. In fact, if cocoa were substituted for the latter, there would be a definite suboptimum level of the thiamine (vitamin B_1) and riboflavin (vitamin B_2) needed for energy conversion, and a considerable lowering of the vitamin A intake.

Appendix: Equipment List

THIS LIST is well worth checking through before each trip; it eliminates that what-have-I-forgotten feeling as you drive toward the trails. Weights are in ounces. You may be able to beat some of them. It pays to try—in added comfort on the trail if not in camp!

To wear

Advisable: Underwear, shirt, socks, trousers, belt, shoes, bandanna, dark glasses, optical glasses (if used), matches, pocket knife.

Optional: Hat or cap, knapsack, watch, lip ointment, notebook and pencil, handkerchief, hunting knife.

To carry

Advisable: Rucksack (56), emergency kit (18), adhesive tape (4), sunburn protection (1), parka (23), sweater (10), bandanna (1), sleeping bag (80), flashlight with new cells (2), wallet and keys (4), cup (3), map (1), toothbrush, soap, and comb in waterproof bag (5), extra clothing: underwear (5), shirt (7), socks (8).

Optional: Air mattress (16), extra glasses and case (3), crash towel (5), mosquito repellent (4), emergency food (12), tent stakes (2), hiking shorts and shirt (16), gloves or mitts (4), shaving kit (6), cigarettes(?), bathing suit.

Community equipment for three or four

Advisable: Waterproof sheet (28), repair kit (18), headlight (22), two nesting pots (16), five spoons (4), extra dark glasses and case (3), toilet tissue, matches, sewing kit (5), food and containers (per man-day) (27–40), campfire permit, compass.

Optional: Tapered tent (64), hand ax and sheath (29), emergency food (32), extra laces (1), can opener (1), light shoes (32), ace bandage (2), shoe wax (6), extra flashlight cells and lamp (10), milk whip (4), playing cards (5), canteen (full) (40), aneroid barometer (3), thermometer (3), first-aid extras (16), shovel (32), foot powder (5), photographic equipment, literature, fishing tackle, musical instruments, and botanical, zoölogical, or geological equipment (weights unpredictable—proceed with care, for the best-intentioned plans for going light can run amuck in these categories; consider the cultural values, of course, but ask yourself, "Can we leave it out?" and try hard to say Yes).

Equipment for rock and ice

The equipment that may be required by those aspiring to more than easy cross-country routes is not nearly so complicated as is the technique required for safe use of the equipment. This book does not cover either subject. See *Manual of Ski Mountaineering.*

First-aid packets

Following are suggestions for packets to be carried on mountain trips.

BACKPACKERS (EACH PERSON)

1½" x 5 yd. adhesive tape
1" roll gauze bandage
6 3" steripads
½ oz. tincture of merthiolate (or substitute 3½ per cent tincture of iodine)

6 capsules codeine sulfate 1 grain with aspirin 5 grains
6 aspirin tablets 5 grains
10 penicillin V tablets, 250 milligrams each
assorted band-aids

ANIMAL PACKERS (FOR PARTY OF 4)

3" x 5 yds. adhesive tape
3 1", 3 2", 3 3" gauze bandages
12 3" steripads
1 oz. tincture of merthiolate
1 large box band-aids

50 aspirin tablets
6 codeine-aspirin
15 penicillin V tablets, 250 milligrams each
2 oz. Kip
2 oz. zinc oxide ointment

NOTE. The best compilation of sources of equipment is the current "Equipment Bulletin" published by the Potomac Appalachian Trail Club, Washington, D.C., supplemented by equipment news items in *Appalachian Trailway News,* published by the Appalachian Trail Conference, 1916 Sunderland Place, N.W., Washington 6, D.C.

Bibliography

BOOKS

American National Red Cross, *American Red Cross First Aid Text-Book* (rev. ed.), Philadelphia.

ATWOOD, WALLACE W., *The Rocky Mountains*, New York, 1945.

BREWER, WILLIAM H., *Up and Down California in 1860–1864* (edited by Francis P. Farquhar), Berkeley and Los Angeles, 1949.

BROWER, DAVID (ed.), *Manual of Ski Mountaineering* (Rev. ed.), San Francisco, 1962.

BUTCHER, DEVEREUX, *Exploring Our National Parks and Monuments*, New York.

CARHART, ARTHUR H., *The Outdoorsman's Cookbook*, New York, 1944.

Department of the Army, *Mountain Operations (FM 70–10)*, prepared under the direction of the Chief of Staff, Washington, D.C., 1960.

EDWARDS, J. GORDON, *A Climber's Guide to Glacier National Park*, San Francisco, 1960.

FARQUHAR, FRANCIS P., "The Literature of Mountaineering," *Appalachia*, Boston, 1939, 1940.

HARRISON, A. E., *Exploring Glaciers—with a Camera*, San Francisco, 1960.

HAZARD, JOSEPH T., *Pacific Crest Trails from Alaska to Cape Horn*, Seattle, 1946.

HENDERSON, KENNETH A., *Handbook of American Mountaineering*, Boston, 1941.

HILDEBRAND, JOEL H. AND LOUISE, *Camp Catering* (2d ed.), New York (Stephen Daye Press), 1941.

KEPHART, HORACE, *Camping and Woodcraft*, New York, 1939.

KING, CLARENCE, *Mountaineering in the Sierra Nevada* (edited and with a preface by Francis P. Farquhar), New York, 1946.

LECONTE, JOSEPH, *A Journal of Ramblings through the High Sierra of California* [in 1875], San Francisco, 1960.

LEOPOLD, ALDO, *A Sand County Almanac and Sketches Here and There*, New York, 1952.

MCDERMAND, CHARLES, *Waters of the Golden Trout Country*, New York, 1946.

———, *Yosemite and Kings Canyon Trout*, New York, 1947.

MANNING, HARVEY (ed.), *Mountaineering: The Freedom of the Hills*, The Mountaineers, Seattle, 1960.

MUIR, JOHN, *My First Summer in the Sierra*, Boston and New York, 1911.

MUSHAM, H. A., *The Technique of the Terrain*, New York, 1944.

ORTENBURGER, LEIGH, *A Climber's Guide to the Teton Range*, San Francisco, 1956.

PEATTIE, RODERICK (ed.), *The Cascades: Mountains of the Pacific Northwest*, New York, 1949.

——— (ed.), *The Inverted Mountains: Canyons of the West*, New York, 1948.

——— (ed.), *The Pacific Coast Ranges*, New York, 1946.

——— (ed.), *The Sierra Nevada: The Range of Light*, New York. 1947.

SAMIVEL, *Sous l'œil des choucas, ou les plaisirs d'alpinisme*, Paris, 1932 [does not require a knowledge of French].

STARR, WALTER A., Jr., *Guide to the John Muir Trail and the High Sierra Region*, San Francisco.

VOGE, HERVEY H. (ed.), *A Climber's Guide to the High Sierra* (2d ptg.), San Francisco, 1956.

WEAVER, ROBERT W. AND ANTHONY F. MERRILL, *Camping Can Be Fun*, New York, 1948.

YOUNG, GEOFFREY W. (ed.), *Mountain Craft*, London, 1947.

JOURNALS

American Alpine Club, New York, *The American Alpine Journal*.

Appalachian Mountain Club, Boston, *Appalachia* (semiannual).

Colorado Mountain Club, Denver, *Trail and Timberline* (monthly).

Mazamas, Portland, Oregon, *Mazama* (monthly, December issue a magazine number).

Mountaineers, Seattle, *The Mountaineer* (monthly, December issue a magazine number).

Potomac Appalachian Trail Club, Washington, D.C., *Bulletin Potomac Appalachian Trail Club* (quarterly).

Sierra Club, San Francisco, *Sierra Club Bulletin* (monthly, annual magazine number).